# JOURNAL FOR THE STUDY OF THE OLD TESTAMENT
## SUPPLEMENT SERIES
# 204

Sheffield Academic Press

# Whose Bible is it Anyway?

## Philip R. Davies

Journal for the Study of the Old Testament
Supplement Series 204

This book is a tribute to my many years of happiness with Birgit,
without whom I would not enjoy biblical scholarship, let alone life.

Copyright © 1995 Sheffield Academic Press

Published by
Sheffield Academic Press Ltd
Mansion House
19 Kingfield Road
Sheffield, S11 9AS
England

Typeset by Sheffield Academic Press
and
Printed on acid-free paper in Great Britain
by Bookcraft
Midsomer Norton, Somerset

British Library Cataloguing in Publication Data

A catalogue record for this book is available
from the British Library

ISBN 1-85075-569-8

CONTENTS

## ACKNOWLEDGMENTS

I ought to thank, for their help in creating this book, all those who heard and commented on those conference papers from which many of the chapters are drawn. I have been both surprised and heartened by the enthusiastic (I do not mean uncritical) interaction that many of them provoked. Of those with whom I have conversed specifically about Chapter 2, I wish to name Meg Davies, my Sheffield colleague, and David Reimer (who now teaches where I was once a student, at Regent's Park College, Oxford). Keith Elliott, of the University of Leeds, and Tom Pattie of the British Library were very helpful with aspects of Chapter 3, and I hope that these friends will not be too ashamed of being associated with the product. Finally, I should acknowledge the editoral assistance of Steve Barganski whose job it has been to see this manuscript turned into a book, on time and in better shape than he got it from me.

# ABBREVIATIONS

| | |
|---|---|
| AB | Anchor Bible (Doubleday) |
| BETL | Bibliotheca ephemeridum theologicarum lovaniensium |
| *BHS* | *Biblia hebraica stuttgartensia* |
| *Bib* | *Biblica* |
| *BR* | *Biblical Research* |
| CRINT | Compendia rerum iudaicarum ad Novum Testamentum |
| *ExpTim* | *Expository Times* |
| *HTR* | *Harvard Theological Review* |
| *JSNT* | *Journal for the Study of the New Testament* |
| JSOTSup | *Journal for the Study of the Old Testament*, Supplement Series |
| *JTS* | *Journal of Theological Studies* |
| KJV | King James Version |
| NIV | New International Version |
| NRSV | New Revised Standard Version |
| OTG | Old Testament Guides |
| *OTS* | *Oudtestamentische Studiën* |
| RSV | Revised Standard Version |
| WBC | Word Biblical Commentary |
| WMANT | Wissenschaftliche Monographien zum Alten und Neuen Testament |
| *ZAW* | *Zeitschrift für die alttestamentliche Wissenschaft* |
| *ZTK* | *Zeitschrift für Theologie und Kirche* |

# Chapter 1

## ABOUT THIS BOOK

Some of the chapters in this book are developed versions of papers written for and read at conferences, and the remainder have been written specially to go with them. One chapter only has already been published, in a less developed form (on the story of Abraham, Chapter 5).

In my last book, *In Search of Ancient Israel*,[1] I was concerned with how the books of the Jewish scriptures came into existence, as a collection, and specifically what societies and social conditions produced them. There I was critical of approaches to such questions that started off from premises derived from the biblical literature itself, especially its own notion of 'Israel', because assuming a historical identity to something that was properly a literary construct is simply bad method. I also suggested that even where biblical scholarship truly aimed at keeping a critical distance from its subject matter, the history and habits of the discourse of 'biblical history' were hard to shake off.

Here I am in a way continuing the debate about method and critical discourse, but dealing with the broader issues of reading entailed in that critique. As with the case of history, it seems to me that one can distinguish in principle between two contexts for a general critical reading strategy of biblical literature. One of these operates 'inside the canon', as it were, and evaluates its subject matter in a way that is predetermined to be ultimately positive; in this reading, where biblical literature equals 'scripture', the critic's job is not to evaluate from a disinterested perspective (or set of perspectives) the values of the text but ultimately to affirm them, in however many different ways: for the contents of bibles are a Good Thing. This goal is largely realized (as it is also predetermined) by the practice of adopting the internal values of the

---

1. *In Search of Ancient Israel* (JSOTSup, 148; repr.; Sheffield: Sheffield Academic Press, 1995).

scriptures as criteria or presuppositions of the 'criticism' (for example that monotheism is a good thing; that this one god, known as Elohim, Yhwh [or whatever] exists, and others do not; that he is just and benevolent; that the world was divinely created; that 'true' and 'false' prophets can be objectively distinguished; that political decisions should be guided by religious considerations, and so on). The goal of such a discourse is to understand more fully its historical, ideological, rhetorical or religious character *to enhance the function of the literature as scripture*. Whatever critical programme this agenda may also wish to serve, it is ultimately serving a confessional purpose.

There is another strategy for the study of biblical literature, which operates 'outside' the canon. This strategy regards the collection and transmission of the contents as part of the reception history of a literature which was created, and given various kinds of authority through time, by the actions of humans, and that these acts of writing and reception are to be evaluated on the same terms as other human acts of writing and reception, just as Jewish and Christian canons are put on an equal footing with other canons of world religions. The values that are adopted in the critique of the literature in this discourse are those adopted by the critical observer and applied to other literature. The critic is free to like or dislike, to pass judgment or refrain, whether out of individual discretion (the prerogative of any reader) or by the application of cultural, philosophical or methodological principles that pertain to the study of ancient literature and ideology generally. What is excluded from this approach is the assumption of a privileged status that the object of study is held intrinsically to merit, and the assumption that the scholar may confine his or her discussion to those who are prepared to make that assumption.

There are some serious issues at stake here involving scholarship itself. Do religious writings make sense to any reader who does not accept the reality of the deities they refer to? Those who believe that the answer is 'yes' for the non-Christian/Jewish scriptures, or of non-Christian/Jewish philosophers (and nearly every academic student of these in the West is a non-believer!) must allow the same for the biblical writings. Do those who claim a religious affinity with a certain body of writings have a better instinct for the meaning of those writings? Do Christians understand the Old Testament better than Jews understand their bible? The problem here is in the phrase 'the meaning': what is 'meaning' and who decides it? In the case of Jewish and Christian readings, the question to be asked is whether the reader can tell a difference between what the text says (or might say) and what the Jewish and Christian interpretative traditions have decided that it says (or should say). If the text (and this might be true to an extent of any text) becomes a prisoner of its own reception, by what strategies can the text be continually liberated?

I shall be arguing that while both 'confessional' and 'non-confessional' approaches to the academic study of the biblical literature may be deemed, in their own way, 'critical', they are nevertheless fundamentally quite different types of behaviour, and they ought not to be confused either in theory or practice. Indeed, the two approaches imply different definitions of the subject matter, and create two different kinds of discourses on biblical matters, and these discourses are so fundamentally divergent as to require and to imply *separate disciplines*.

The issue of which of these two perspectives is more proper, or correct, is generating an ongoing battle. The issue also has a certain 'political' dimension. Different parties have an interest in the contents of bibles and what should be done with them, and they often take to squabbling or at least sniping about whose interest is the more authentic. My suggestion is that any such conflict is misconceived and unnecessary, because there is no common space that they can both legitimately occupy; rather, each should recognize, cherish and cultivate its own identity and operate within its own separate territory, without coveting its neighbour's house.

That is not to say, however, that the choice between the two disciplines of 'biblical studies' and 'scripture' is an indifferent one. There are ethical and methodological questions entailed in the option for one or other. There are, after all, several agents with a stake in the 'meaning' of the biblical books: the reader, the writer(s) and the institutions for whom a bible is a sacred book. In a very obvious sense, the religious institutions and communities of Judaism and Christianity have a claim on their bibles. This claim is valid within those communities, but to try and universalize it is to deny that these bibles should play any part in study of the cultures of the ancient Mediterranean world, or of Western culture, whose domains include but also extend beyond church or synagogue. Moreover, the writings in bibles also have readers who, inside or outside the church, are individual human beings, like the authors they are reading, and there is long history of individual readings, even by Christians, that are not 'ecclesial' (e.g. Dante, Blake, Eliot). Just as there is a need to articulate the role and meaning of the scriptures in the context of Judaism and Christianity, so there is no realistic hope of imposing an ecclesial interpretation outside the ecclesial domain. Whatever communication may be possible between writer and reader via private reading of the text cannot be censored or controlled by an intervening history of ecclesiastical reading (or readings). Finally, no ancient writer should have his or her text accorded a retrospective meaning dictated by the dogmatic requirements of an institution that chose to 'canonize' it. The discourse of the church about its scriptures, then, belongs within the church domain, and cannot be extended beyond it. Nor does it need to—or so I shall argue.

Hence, while the right to a 'confessional' discourse about the scriptures must be upheld, it cannot claim a jurisdiction over how bibles are to be defined and read outside its own bounds. But as part of the necessary separation of interests in biblical study, a non-confessional discourse must also define itself properly. The bulk of the chapters in this book are an exercise in definition through practice. The fundamental issue, and the subject of the third chapter, is how the object of study is to be construed. What *is* a 'bible', viewed from outside the church or synagogue? The fourth chapter tries to formulate an answer: it is a particular kind of literary artifact, and indeed, one that cannot strictly be referred to in the singular. There is no one 'Bible', but several 'bibles'. (The use of the singular must always imply the question: 'whose bible?'—hence the title of this book, which is not meant to be provocative, but simply and pedantically precise.)

Another area where a 'non-confessional' discourse needs to assert its own principles is in speaking of the deity. It is common in all academic biblical writing to speak of 'God' (or 'the Lord'); that is after all how English bibles usually render the various Hebrew and Greek terms, since they are books of scripture. The assumption of this usage, however, is that this 'God' is extra-textual, that the term refers to a metaphysical entity whose existence and attributes are conceded and known by the critics as well as the authors of the scriptures. Or at least it accords some privilege to this deity over deities that other humans have worshipped and still do. To continue to use such terms, even in inverted commas, runs the risk of implying that what the ancient writers meant by *Elohim* or *Yhwh* or *theos*, and what they can have him do in their stories, or how they construct him in their petitions will conform essentially to the definitions of a modern Christian or Jewish believer whose deity has been defined over centuries by not only the scriptures but also such ideas as those of Stoicism, Neoplatonism, mediaeval scholasticism, rabbinism, mysticism, Hasidism and much else. It is therefore more precise, and less misleading, to refer to 'Yhwh' or 'Elohim' or 'the deity' or 'the god' without prejudice as to its existence or character beyond what the text portrays. To many this may seem pedantic. It is, and pedantry is the essence of criticism; it is also usages of this kind that can define the character of an entire discourse. These things are neither petty nor irrelevant. It is very important to remember that we are not describing, or disputing about, someone that *you* may believe and *I* do not, but about the creation of ancient writers whose own religious experience, and literary artistry, will have been very different from ours. In Chapters 4, 5 and 7, this deity is treated, as I believe is proper, as a character in a story, not because of some atheistic prejudice I have, but because *that is how the writers of these texts wanted it to be*. Whether their private beliefs about deities corresponded exactly to what they wrote about depends on whether or not we treat them seriously as creative writers. I see no reason to insist that biblical storytellers, any more than modern ones, feel obliged to write only what they themselves hold to be true.

A word is needed, finally, about avoiding the term 'biblical text' or 'biblical writer'. The former is extremely convenient and any circumlocution will appear clumsy. But the implication of the usage is that 'biblical' imparts some essence to the texts it contains. It is also potentially confusing: can we call 1 Maccabees a biblical text? Certainly: it is in several bibles that I own. But it is not biblical for a Protestant. And *1 Enoch* or *Jubilees*? These are in other peoples' bibles. So long as the phrase 'biblical text' refers in a convenient shorthand way to no more than any text that we can find in a bible, it is a neutral and accurate description. If I use the phrase in this book from time to time, that is what I intend it to mean. 'Biblical writer' I shall, however, avoid, because of its anachronism. No bible ever had an author or writer. Bibles are volumes of collected works, all written before anything like a 'bible' was conceived. As a shorthand for an author whose work happens to be found in a bible it is perhaps defensible, but I remain uneasy about the juxtaposition of the terms 'author' and 'bible'; there is nothing in the term 'biblical' that tells us anything useful about the author, except that his or her work was taken up later into someone's canon. I certainly doubt that most authors (there might be the odd exception, like ben Sira or the writer of 1 Maccabees) write (or could have written) with the aim of contributing to a 'canon', and far less a 'bible'. I therefore avoid the term 'biblical writer/author/narrator', and encourage others interested in non-confessional scholarship to do the same.

The contents of this book, then, deal with, and try to apply, the principles of a self-consciously non-confessional discourse, with topics relating to the characterization of the deity Yhwh (alias Elohim, at least sometimes?), and, in the case of Chapter 6, with the way in which ancient writers have made use of the notion of a deity to defer ethical responsibilities that *we* would have had them assume themselves. I hope to be showing at points during these studies that non-confessional readings, which offer negative as well as positive evaluations of the ethics, aesthetics and other literary ideologies of biblical texts, are no less ethically and intellectually challenging than those which seek to explore the confessional Christian or Jewish dimensions. Being humanistic about scriptures and agnostic about deities does not deprive one of a sense of right and wrong. Nor does it diminish one's joy in reading a bible. It is meant to encourage bible reading, not to restrict it. And if it is possible (as I think it is) to write 'theologically' without invoking gods as real presences, then this is a book about theology. But most of all it is written in the belief that ancient authors, their texts, modern readers and academic scholarship are all in need of continual liberation from their own idolatry. And 'the Bible' is one of the greatest idols of modern times.

### Additional Note

Those readers who dislike theoretical and philosophical arguments can leave out Chapter 2, which is rather long and even tedious, unless you believe that biblical studies has to do with theology. In which case, to be fair to me and yourselves, you had better plough through it.

Chapter 2

## TWO NATIONS, ONE WOMB

Two nations are in your womb, and two peoples born of you shall be distinguished: one shall be stronger than the other; the elder shall serve the younger (Gen. 25.23)

### *Church,[1] Theology, Academy*

The front flap of a recent book[2] displays the challenging words 'should biblical studies continue to exclude theological concerns from its agenda?' This statement puzzled me, and on my next visit to the university library I scanned the bookshelves. I did the same in my own study. As I had expected, a very large number of the books in both locations devoted to biblical studies are explicitly or implicitly theological in their agenda, interest or intended audience. Of the publishers' catalogues I receive, more than half contain books on biblical studies alongside or among books of theology or even of devotional literature. Although the recent upsurge in non-theological studies of the Bible, including ideological criticism and deconstruction, has created a very significant minority, books and articles devoted to theological treatments of 'the Bible' exceed them numerically in output. At conferences devoted to biblical studies, such as meetings of the Society of Biblical Literature or Catholic Biblical Association or the British Society for Old Testament Study, a large number of papers and sessions deal with

---

1. In much of this chapter I shall be dealing with 'church' rather than 'synagogue'. The reasons are that in some cases what applies to the church does not apply to the synagogue, and that the debating partners I have chosen represent Christian and not Jewish positions. Where relevant, I shall try to include Judaism explicitly in my discussion; otherwise Jewish readers, or readers interested in Judaism, may add 'the synagogue' to this text wherever they find it appropriate.

2. F. Watson, *Text, Church and World* (Edinburgh: T. & T. Clark; Grand Rapids: Eerdmans, 1994).

theological themes. Still, rightly or wrongly, some concern is apparently being felt that theology is being shouldered aside or in some way deprivileged in recent biblical scholarship.

Such a concern has in fact been around for some time. In 1971 Christopher Evans published a book entitled *'Is Holy Scripture Christian?' and Other Questions.*[3] In his inaugural lecture at Oxford in 1978, James Barr asked whether study of the bible belonged to theology.[4] Evans was concerned to protect 'academic' study from theological claims that were not capable of being critically tested, while Barr came to the more eirenic conclusion that biblical studies neither has to belong to theology nor has to be separate, and recommended that the sometimes uneasy juxtaposition of churchly and scholarly interests called not for any 'revolutionary change' but for 'understanding and acceptance'.[5] Both Evans and Barr make explicit that the issue of biblical studies and theology is at the same time an issue of church and academy. But while Evans stresses the differences between the two sides and their values, Barr seems content that theology should share with non-theological interests what is either a neutral discipline or one that lends itself to more than one approach.

The matter was raised again in 1989 by a successor of Barr in Oxford, John Barton, who observed that

> there is a widespread perception of professional biblical scholarship as concerned only to talk to itself, taking the Bible away from the believing community and encapsulating it in a small world with its own rules. The Bible, people feel, needs to be given back to the church.

He added, referring to the Old Testament, that there are 'lay people who feel that the specialists ought to be helping Christians to understand this major part of the Christian Bible better...' A little later he commented on biblical scholarship: 'where, we are asked, is its commitment to Christian faith and to the life of the churches and their members'?[6]

---

3.   C.F. Evans, *'Is Holy Scripture Christian?' and Other Questions* (London: SCM Press, 1971).

4.   In his inaugural address as Oriel Professor in Oxford (*Does Biblical Study Still Belong to Theology?* [Oxford: Clarendon Press, 1978]).

5.   *Does Biblical Study Still Belong to Theology?*, p. 17.

6.   J. Barton, 'Should Old Testament Study be more Theological', *ExpTim* 100 (1989), pp. 443-48; quotes from pp. 443 and 444.

It might seem strange to some professional academic biblical scholars (and Barton, being one himself, quite properly acknowledges this in his article) that 'people' should think the academy should be studying 'the Bible' in order to serve the Christian church. But Barton's article appeared in a journal, the *Expository Times*, which is published for the clergy. His primary audience, I infer, was an ecclesiastical one. The somewhat one-sided language of 'taking the Bible away' and 'encapsulating it in a small world with its own rules' (as if this could not be said of 'the church' itself!) and the assumption that biblical scholarship ought to be serving churches and their members probably found an echo among many of the regular readers.

Now, the notion that academic biblical studies and church commitments belong naturally together is not uncommon within the academy either. The *Expository Times* (a well-edited and widely-read journal) is found among the periodicals in many university libraries (including my own institution's), among the same stacks as academic journals. It reviews academic books as well as offering sermon notes, and seems to advertise very successfully that church and academy belong together and get on well together. No doubt many of its readers are people who work as both scholars and clergy, who lecture on weekdays and preach or worship on Sundays.

Nevertheless, my contention is that all these treatments misrepresent the issue, though not wilfully. Although there is certainly an overlap between the categories theology/non-theology and church/academy, they are not symmetrical alternatives. Academic theology exists largely *outside* the church. Very few churches *appoint* theologians; it is not an ecclesiastical office (the Catholic church is one of a few exceptions, and these persons are drawn mainly from orders such as the Jesuits or Dominicans). Their clergy may *study* academic theology, but how far do they apply it in their ministry? Any more than they use their Hebrew or Greek? Church discourse is not inevitably theological, as distinct from being devotional or pastoral. Church and academy do not share on the whole a common discourse or common interests. Churchgoers are not greatly bothered about academic theology (most of them are probably unorthodox in one or other respect, anyway). In other words, 'theology' and 'the church' are not necessarily the same thing, and the issue of church and academy should not be confused with the issue of humanistic scholarship versus theology.

*Church and Academy*

The difference of interest between church and academy is, in my opinion, not really a problem to either side—or need not be. Most people may well think that Christian belief is the natural virtue of a biblical scholar. Some may expect professors to preach in the classroom, or may expect a lecture from the pulpit (neither of these occasions is unknown). But very many know, even if only roughly, the difference of interest between a preacher and a scholar. And most church people, in my experience, find it easy enough to appreciate the distinction between what an academy does and what a church does. The problem is that people (academic biblical scholars especially) do not take the trouble to explain it to them. Indeed, on the contrary, they write books that presuppose precisely that overlap of interest. Scholars who earn PhDs and write devotional books may well convey the impression that competence in scholarship delivers authority in pastoral matters and questions of Christian belief. But it is a mischievous impression. As a general principle, scholarship does not make a better religious believer, nor religious belief a better scholar.

A fitting term is needed for what church (or synagogue) members do in their religious communities, with their bibles. I shall use (as do many churchgoers) 'bible study'. The purpose of 'bible study' is religious understanding of scripture, and the presupposition of this activity is that the bible of the church or synagogue relates directly to the life of its members in an authoritative way. It is a divine message for them. Such study may occasionally draw on academic methods or resources (e.g. learning about the chronology of Paul's missionary journeys or the geography of ancient Palestine) but these are ancillary and of themselves bring no deepening of *religious* understanding. 'Bible study', which takes place within the context of devotion, is not really about ancient Middle Eastern history or geography, or about time and place of authorship, or stylistics, or chronology. Whether or not Paul wrote Ephesians, or David wrote any Psalms, or what law-book if any Ezra may have had in his hand do not directly address the concerns of this bible study. The history of the text or of the canon, the structure of the Hebrew language, the origin of the genre of 'apocalypse' are of no *intrinsic* interest to people *as church members*. Academic biblical studies is incidental, accessory to synagogue or church interests, even though individual members may have a lively interest in academic questions.

Academic study, for which I reserve the term 'biblical studies', by contrast *is* interested in how and why biblical literature came to be written, in the constraints and nuances of the original languages, the history of transmission of text and canon. It is by contrast uninvolved in questions of authority or inspiration, since it has no tools for addressing such matters: they cannot be formulated or resolved by academic discourse; at best such claims can only be described and analysed. It can study whether Abraham is likely to have lived or whether there are three collections within the book of Isaiah, but it is not competent to draw implications for the existence of Yhwh, the validity of 'prophetic' claims or the status of the bible as a religious document for Jews or Christians. These matters fall outside its competence.

Put this way, the separate interests of church and academy in 'the Bible' are easy enough to distinguish. There is no real danger of confusing what is done with bibles in church on Sabbaths or Sundays and what is done on weekdays in university classrooms. The same people can easily indulge in both, so long as they do not try and do both at the same time. 'Church vs. academy' is an issue because there are those people who for reasons of their own want to involve it in what is really a debate about two different approaches to study of bibles/'the Bible' that claim to be 'academic'. For *that* reason we shall need to return to the domains of church and academy later on in this chapter.

*Theology and Non-theology*
Let us use the term 'biblical studies' for an academic discourse on bibles. This term is in fact used to describe both autonomous university *departments* (which are still relatively rare) and sub-divisions within university departments or Faculties of Theology. The former will tend to be embraced within a Faculty of Arts or a Humanities School, a School of Religion or of Philosophy. However, within the traditional academic discipline called 'theology' exists what is called 'scripture' (or possibly 'Old Testament' and 'New Testament'). These sections are also in some instances being called 'biblical studies'. But in this latter case the change of nomenclature is potentially misleading, for as long as these academic sections function like 'scripture', that is as a branch of theology, they differ from the 'biblical studies' that exists outside theology. Now, where 'biblical studies' is a constituent discipline of a school of something other than theology, there is no reason at all why the discipline should be theological in anything other than a descriptive sense (by which token,

biblical studies is as much 'literature'). Whether this non-theological 'biblical studies' is a different discipline within a School of Religion or Philosophy is an interesting question, and I am not concerned to deny that there may be significant distinctions. But between all these and theological biblical studies (i.e. 'scripture') lies a basic distinction which for my purposes is the important one, and it is the distinction between a confessional and a non-confessional approach. Where academic study of 'the Bible'/bibles is concerned, there is such a difference between theology and non-theology (let us give it a proper name at least: 'humanism' or 'humanities') that I cannot see it helpful to use the same name for both. It would be much better for us to distinguish between 'biblical studies' (humanistic) and 'scripture' (theological).

If this naming were insisted upon (and the distinction that it quite clearly signifies), I doubt that either those who represent the discipline of theology or others would protest. So let us, indeed, insist upon it, and consider the disputed questions that have been alluded to in the light of this nomenclature. 'Should biblical scholars address essentially the theology of the Bible'? 'What is the place of religious faith in biblical scholarship'? Such formulations assume one of two things: *either* that there is a 'proper' conduct of academic biblical studies which ought to be theological or non-theological; *or* there is a common discipline of biblical scholarship within which the sides can and should reach an accommodation. But if there is no single academic *discipline*, there is no necessary 'common ground' between theology and non-theology. There are, instead, two separate disciplines, each of which has a different definition of what it is that is being studied; indeed, each construes 'bible' as a different object of investigation. This difference, indeed, is neatly represented in the alternatives 'the Bible' and 'bibles'—a distinction unfortunately obliterated by the use of the adjective 'biblical'.

So even though both 'scripture' and 'biblical studies' appear to an outsider to be examining the same thing, namely a book with the name 'Bible' on its cover, in fact they are not. A *discipline* is not the same thing as a *subject area* like 'bible'—or else astronomy and astrology would be the same discipline, as would alchemy and chemistry. A discipline is defined by a methodology, by aims, practices and presuppositions. Chemistry and physics both deal with the nature of matter, as do sociologists and historians at times. But do they share presuppositions, methods, practices and aims? It might be argued that chemistry and physics often converge, and that they are both aspects of a larger 'natural science', perhaps to be subsumed under some Unified Theory. They are, if you like, branches of 'pure science'. But under what 'unified theory' regarding bibles might theology and non-theology converge?[7] If there were such a domain, it would be valid to argue about the place of theology in 'biblical studies'. But since there is not, 'scripture' and 'biblical studies' must be, and be seen as, separate disciplines focusing on more or less the same material, though in each case differently defined.

Within 'scripture', though not within 'biblical studies', some of the presuppositions of the religious discourse of the church are legitimately taken over: indeed, only within the church does the term 'scripture' make any sense, since theology does not study scriptures other than those of the religion whose theology it is dealing with (that is the business of yet another discipline, religious studies). Thus, within 'scripture' bibles are sources of inspiration, they are authoritative, they talk about a real being referred to as 'God', they contain the propositions from which Christian doctrine is derived, and so on. The end point of the discipline of 'scripture' is the definition or clarification of the theology of a particular religion. It is thus confessional. It may adopt many of the features of a non-confessional academic discourse: interest in historical research, the history of the 'canon', authorship and dating of biblical books, the 'Synoptic problem' the 'historical Jesus' and so on, but the ultimate *object* of this discipline is integration within the broader concerns of theology: the appropriation of whatever conclusions are reached to the question of scriptural status and authority. Its conclusions are circumscribed in advance by credal considerations. Now, one may want to argue that a non-confessional discipline of 'biblical studies' is credally predetermined in a similar way. But I do not believe that this case can be made, and I am not going to try and suggest its arguments. For even if such a case *could* be made, my point remains valid: these different presupposition, being non-negotiable, would require separate disciplines.

---

7.   A purely 'descriptive' 'biblical theology', for example, is no solution, because such an exercise makes sense only within a theological agenda. From a non-theological point of view such an exercise would be merely a catalogue of statements with no obvious value. Even from a perspective of 'religious studies' such a thing as 'biblical theology' would comprise a valid object only insofar as it was an expression of the way in which scripture functions within the religious systems of Christianity, and not because of any *intrinsic* worth.

To sum up what has been said so far: the dichotomies of church/academy and theology/biblical studies are not interchangeable. For there are *three* arenas of bible study. One is the church, which, as a confessing community, requires its Bible for devotional and liturgical purposes; as far as doctrinal purposes go, it is rare to find any church studying its bible in the context of systematic theology: the level at which scripture informs doctrine among churchgoers is relatively *un*theological, in fact. A second arena is the 'biblical studies' of the academy, which is humanistic and non-confessional (and which I shall define a bit more fully in due course). A third is 'Scripture', which is that subdiscipline of theology that deals with 'the Bible'. This discipline exists *physically* within the domain of the academy but serves the church, or claims to. This summary makes it clear that the problem is not with the church or with biblical studies but with 'theology', in whose interests it is, generally speaking, to resist the separation of church and academic studies, because to accede to this separation would raise interesting but probably unpleasant questions regarding the very status of theology both as an academic subject and as a useful contributor to church life.

Church and academy, then, operate in separate domains, to different ends, and are not incompatible because they are not commensurate. 'Scripture' and 'biblical studies' are a more difficult issue, because (1) they are commonly perceived, both inside and outside the academy, to be one and the same academic discipline and (2) it is in the interests of one of these ('scripture') that this distinction be concealed. These are my 'two nations' vying within the womb of the academy. In combining elements of a non-confessional discourse with elements of a confessional one, 'scripture' both claims to represent the interests of the church (which, as I have said, I actually doubt) while also claiming a right to the ground occupied by the non-confessional discipline of biblical studies. It is this discipline of 'scripture' that needs most of all to be 'outed': not rejected or devalued, but understood for what it is: a 'confessional-critical' discipline, and certainly not to be confused with non-confessional academic biblical studies.

*Discourse*
The task of following up the conceptual distinction between scripture and biblical studies is complicated by institutional habit. Both disciplines share to a large extent the same social space, very often employ the

same personnel, and produce similar-looking books and journals.[8] Indeed, this institutional overlap has given rise to the problem that has provoked this chapter: the employment of a common 'discourse', at once potentially critical and potentially confessional. The term 'discourse' can be used in a number of technical senses, and 'discourse analysis' covers a set of sub-disciplines in linguistics, philosophy and sociology.[9] As I use the term here, 'discourse' means communication governed by a set of conventions agreed between the participants, conventions that do not have to be specified but are either carried by signals in the communication itself or indicated by external contexts. Discourse defines particular groupings who, in using it, identify themselves with its user-group and implicitly or explicitly exclude others from that group. Choice of discourse is a form of social identification, and discourses can represent groups such as social classes, enthusiasts, males or females, racial minorities, members of a profession and elites. Each discourse also conveys or implies an ideology that defines the 'community' that shares and possesses that discourse, and reflect its 'social world', the reality that it constructs around itself, which can be called its 'ideology'. One of the major debates in discourse analysis is whether an ideology-free discourse is possible, and how, since we are all bound to use *some* discourse whenever we speak, we are able to converse with others using a different discourse.[10] This debate obviously raises the question—which I will consider at the end of this chapter—as to whether certain kinds of discourse are more 'inclusive' than others, and thus engage a wider

8.    Interestingly, while the work of academic biblical studies is often to be found in explicitly 'theological' journals, I know of no journal that is explicitly devoted to humanistic and non-confessional biblical studies, though there are at least two biblical journals that *in practice* reject work that belongs clearly to the discipline of 'scripture'.

9.    The sense in which I am using the term owes something to the following: L. Althusser ('Ideology and Ideological State Apparatuses', in *Lenin and Philosophy and Other Essays* [New York: Monthly Review Press, 1971], pp. 127-86), M. Foucault (cf. his *The Archaeology of Knowledge* [New York: Harper & Row, 1972], J. Habermas (*Knowledge and Human Interests* [Boston: Beacon Press, 1975], H.G. Gadamer (*Truth and Method* [New York: Seabury Press, 1975]) and P. Ricoeur (*Time and Narrative* [3 vols.; Chicago: Chicago University Press, 1984–88]). The positions of these writers regarding the role and extent of 'discourse' and its relation to ideology differ considerably, but the last three in particular have been in conversation.

10.    This issue is prominent in the debate between Habermas, who thinks that ideology-free discourse is ideally achievable, and Gadamer, who disagrees.

community and exclude fewer potential participants.

Another very important aspect of discourse is its facility to act as a vehicle for power. By forcing a debate into a particular discourse, people are able to control the way in which they (and their conversants) speak about 'reality' (or, in this particular case, 'the Bible' or 'bibles'). Thus, to take a non-biblical example, 'the economy' is one way in which politicians, bankers and journalists talk about what others experience as personal living standards. But these terms are not value-free. Whether one speaks of a 'citizen' or a 'customer' or a 'client' is not a matter of indifference, for while one person may be each of these, the terminology implies different rights and responsibilities: 'customers', for example, can only be customers if they pay, and so poor people, who are included when one speaks a political and social discourse that includes 'citizens', are excluded when the discourse of buying and selling is applied to the political and social sphere.[11] Discourses are not neutral, innocent or equal.

'Biblical studies' and 'scripture' ought to have their own separate discourses. Bible/bibles, God/god, faith/religion are merely verbal examples: the difference is whether or what you confess. The theological discipline of 'scripture', though operating within the academy, typically assumes that 'the Bible' belongs to the church, while a non-theological discipline will typically argue that 'bibles' are a genre of cultural phenomena. One implies that the Bible is revelation, the other that bibles are products of human literary creativity. But like Jacob and Esau, those practising scripture or biblical studies tend to assume, or assert, that there is only one birthright, and thus to understand themselves as competing for the same thing. One reason for this is that they are mostly not consciously aware of doing one as distinct from the other. So many biblical scholars assume that there is only one proper way to study 'the Bible'/bibles academically, namely their own. While a good deal of blurring can be done, ultimately the differences of discourse cannot be resolved by the victory of one over another. It is possible to pursue a critical study of both 'bibles' and 'the Bible', to speak of 'God' and of 'the deity Yhwh', so long as each follows its own separate track. Any mixture of the two ceases to be critical.[12] This is because of the need for

11. This impressive example was given by Tony Benn, MP, in the Sheffield Academic Press lecture at the University of Sheffield, 17 March 1995.

12. I attempted to formulate my view in a rudimentary way in 'Do Old Testament Studies Need a Dictionary', in D.J.A. Clines, S.A. Fowl and S.E. Porter (eds.), *The Bible in Three Dimensions. Essays in Celebration of Forty Years of Biblical Studies*

a coherent world-view to justify the particular discipline being pursued. Behind the humanistic and theological disciplines lie not only different interest groups but different views of the world (theistic/materialist) and different evaluations of 'bible' (revelation, literary artifact).

We cannot have a *single* discipline in which radically different accounts of how the world works, what human are here for, what knowledge is, how truth is sought, and so on, can mix together. A single 'biblical scholarship' cannot coexist unless common criteria for evaluation, use of language and philosophy are in place. It would seem to me self-evident that a confessional discourse and a non-confessional one cannot possibly combine to form a single discourse. A non-confessional one would be what is often called by its opponents 'positivistic'. This means in effect that it is based on evidence that is public and accessible, in logical arguments applied to the evidence, in non-contradiction, in replacing belief by judgment and insisting that conclusions follow freely from evidence and argument, and are not judged by 'orthodoxy'. The confessional discourse of 'scripture' has, by virtue of its acceptance of a canon of sacred writings, based its entire procedure on a matter of religious commitment and not an empirical fact. It can only be 'critical' insofar as it maintains coherence within the committed bounds of what is confessed. But as long as in practice a single discourse appears to operate, the obvious separation of 'scripture' and 'biblical studies' can be ignored or resisted.

### Emics and Etics

So far I have merely claimed that two different disciplines of biblical study are actually juxtaposed in the 'academy', where their respective discourses mingle rather freely. I have hinted at their characteristics, and noted a few, but I have not attempted to analyse them or their mingling. It is now time to show some examples. I propose to undertake a critique of specific texts. Each has been chosen so as to illustrate the *disguised* interplay of different discourses and interests within a single piece of academic writing. The examples will also furnish key indexes by which the different discourses and their interests identify themselves. I begin with what I think is the easiest index: canon.

*in the University of Sheffield* (JSOTSup, 87; Sheffield: JSOTS Press, 1990), pp. 321-35.

*Canon*

In reviewing the history of 'Old Testament Introduction', Brevard Childs offered the following critique of the genre as it has been developed:

> In the first place, the historical Introduction as it has developed since Eichhorn does not have for its goal the analysis of the canonical literature of the synagogue and church, but rather it seeks to describe the history of the development of the Hebrew literature and to trace the earlier and later stages of the history. As a result, there always remains an enormous hiatus between the description of the critically reconstructed literature and the actual canonical text which has been received and used as authoritative scripture by the community.
>
> Secondly, because of the predominantly historical interest, the critical Introduction usually fails to understand the peculiar dynamics of Israel's religious literature, which has been greatly influenced by the process of establishing the scope of the literature, forming its particular shape, and structuring its inner relationships.
>
> Thirdly, the usual historical critical Introduction has failed to relate the nature of the literature correctly to the community which treasured it as scripture. It is constitutive of Israel's history that the literature formed the identity of the religious community which in turn shaped the literature. This fundamental dialectic which lies at the heart of the canonical process is lost when the critical Introduction assumes that a historically referential reading of the Old Testament is the key to its interpretation.[13]

Childs's 'canonical' approach to the Old Testament has been the object both of great praise and of stringent criticism.[14] It remains, however, a popular and productive way of practising biblical criticism which, through Childs's students and followers, exerts a considerable influence on biblical studies. His account of what study of the Old Testament should be, then, is an appropriate choice for analysis. My interest here is not to rehearse the merits or otherwise of his 'canonical' method but to examine the discourse of the passage just quoted. Childs prompts us in the right direction by setting up a distinction between 'historical-critical' investigation of the Old Testament, which concentrates

---

13. B. Childs, *Introduction to the Old Testament as Scripture* (Philadelphia: Westminster Press; London: SCM Press, 1979), pp. 40-41.

14. See, e.g., the collection of essays in *JSOT* 16 (1980); J. Barr, *Holy Scripture: Canon, Authority, Criticism* (Oxford: Clarendon Press, 1983), pp. 130-71. A particularly useful and important critique is to be found in M.G. Brett, *Biblical Criticism in Crisis? The Impact of the Canonical Approach on Old Testament Studies* (Cambridge: Cambridge University Press, 1991); Watson, *Text, Church and World*, pp. 30-45.

on the early stages of the history of production of the text, and a method which focuses on the text itself as produced, and received, by 'the community' in the form of a canon. These alternatives are presented at one level as being concerned with how the Old Testament was historically produced, and thus Childs's method is represented as a historical one. Elsewhere in the same book he says,

> In sum, the issue is not whether or not an Old Testament Introduction should be historical, but the nature of the historical categories being applied...It is a basic misunderstanding of the canonical approach to describe it as a non-historical reading of the Bible. Nothing could be further from the truth![15]

Indeed, Childs in effect charges historical criticism with not being *adequately* historical: the 'historical-critical' approach *fails to understand* the real historical process in the formation of the Old Testament. The missing, key factor is the 'religious dynamic'[16] consisting of the interaction between community and text.

It looks at first sight, then, as if we have a debate between Childs and his targets on common ground, using a common discourse. Childs anyway appears to think so, because he insists that the issue is not between 'liberal' and 'conservative' or 'scientific' and 'ecclesiastical' or 'objective' and 'confessional', but relates to the nature of the canon—a matter, he agrees, of *historical* understanding. He is certainly claiming that his discourse and that of the 'historical critics' is one and the same. For him, the difference is simply between a historical approach that addresses the Old Testament as a set of ancient texts, and one that recognizes the text as a canon, in its formation as well as in its completion. Thus, he introduces the notion of the 'canonical process', the shaping of the text within a community inspired by a 'religious dynamic'. In making this claim he is appealing, if I understand him correctly, to an objective historical fact, and not to a religious commitment or to an ideal.

But is this what is really going on? Not at all, because Childs does not carry out his argument according to historical methodologies, according to the way in which an academic historian would proceed. There is no investigation of the 'canonical process' and no documentation for his assertion that such a thing took place. In the course of his work, Childs

15. *Introduction to the OT as Scripture*, pp. 41, 71.
16. *Introduction to the OT as Scripture*, p. 41.

certainly makes many perceptive literary and ideological links within the books of the Old Testament, which make an interesting extension of the redaction-critical procedures of the 'historical critics'. But the links *between* the books, which is where the weight of his canon-based hermeneutic must fall, are problematic. What does he make of the fact that the Jewish scriptures did not have a regular order, and existed as individual scrolls, not collected into a single book until the Middle Ages? He says that the 'canonical process' is 'constitutive of Israel's history', but *what* history of Israel is he reading? What community or communities, precisely, *did* 'shape' the text, and by what mechanism did it/they do it? *How* in fact is a canonical shape actually imposed?

To all these rather vital questions there may be all sorts of answers, and certainly one could suggest kinds of evidence that might be sought to confirm or refute the hypothesis of a process of canonical shaping. But it is very significant that Childs is either unable, or does not bother, to argue in the way that his targets do. His claim that the 'historical critics' have failed to take canon seriously involves him in making assertions about the Old Testament that are 'historical' because they assert something about the past—but they are not 'historical' assertions in the sense that they are arrived at by any historical methodology. They are simply dogmas.

Lest it be thought I am unfair, let me persevere. In theory one might at least be able to investigate whatever evidence is relevant to a possible 'canonical process'. But this is not true of Childs's appeal to a 'religious dynamic'. He sees this as the key to the process of formation of the Old Testament, that the 'historical critics' have failed to understand. But here he is invoking something that lies beyond historical comprehension or evaluation. In what way might a *historical* mode of enquiry identify and illuminate this dynamic? None of the targetted critics denied that the writings were inspired by religious motives. What more are they supposed to say? It might not be unfair to conclude that Childs is criticizing historical-critical scholarship for being historical (and critical)! The implication of this is that he is going beyond what can be called 'historical' criticism. For while apparently engaging his targets at the level of history, he is really accusing them of ignoring aspects that cannot be comprehended by a historical approach. Both 'canon' and 'religious dynamic' are terms that *belong to a different kind of discourse* and invoke different kinds of presuppositions, onto which Childs is, consciously or not, moving the ground of debate. In that discourse, the word 'canon' plays a key, and ambiguous, role, as will presently be explained.

My comments made about the 'canonical process' apply also when Childs turns from the creation of the canon to its reception. He rightly criticizes historical criticism for paying too much attention to the processes of formation of the Old Testament and too little to the history of its reception. (As I shall observe in Chapter 3, most of this agenda deals with the time before there *is* any bible at all). Here again his agenda *seems* to be historical; here again, however, we find no historical argumentation. How did *various* Christian canons come into being? How and why do the various 'communities' for whom bibles function as a canon differ? Is 'canon' viewed the same way in every Christian church? Childs has been particularly and repeatedly criticized for taking as his Old Testament canon the most recent of all (the fifteenth-century Protestant one), which corresponds in content to the Jewish canon, if there is such a thing, but not to any early Christian canon. The reception of the canon in the church is evidently a matter of *process*, but a process irrelevant to Childs's 'canonical' approach. Paradoxically, he *refuses* to deal with a canonical process for the last two thousand years! He insists on canon as a historical fact, but actually de-historicizes it, idealizing it as a set of texts independent of any particular church at any particular time.[17] At the end of this analysis, then, we can say that while Childs is apparently discoursing at the level of 'history', mimicking a critical approach, he is actually *uninterested* in historical processes, and unable or unconcerned to bother with historical argumentation. His 'canon' is not a historical product at all, but a confessional datum. Playing with two different disciplines allows Childs to get away with an entirely bogus claim: a dogma posing as a historical hypothesis.

The clearest evidence of the 'double-discourse' that is going on is in the title of Childs's book: 'Introduction to the Old Testament as Scripture'. 'As Scripture' says it all, or should do. But instead of simply asserting that he is writing as a church member and offering a programme for Christian study of the Old Testament which recognizes its status as scripture, Childs tries to colonialize study of 'the Bible' and expel methods that do not deal with 'scripture' as a confessed datum by arguing that 'canon' and 'scripture' are actually 'facts' that no-one can deny. Nor, I suppose, should we overlook 'Old Testament'; this is another 'confessional' term, and one rather inappropriate for a writer

17. A point made by Brett, *Biblical Criticism in Crisis*, pp. 13-14.

who is adopting a Jewish canon. It would be churlish to blame Childs for the widespread use of this term, but equally it would be hard to find a more incongruous instance.

Note, then, how the discourse switches during the argument. (1) The Old Testament is *in fact* a canon/scripture (or more correctly a part of a canon). (2) As canon/scripture it was self-evidently brought into being by a religious community. (3) It belongs within the believing community that created and cherishes it as authoritative. (4) Therefore the proper way to approach the Old Testament is from a perspective that acknowledges that canon as authoritative, that is as scripture. The argument (pseudo-argument, in fact) thus moves from a historical assertion that these books are in fact in the form of a canon to the theological conclusion that therefore only from the point of view of a confessing community can it properly be understood, that is *as it historically is*!

But Childs is not concerned with whether the production of the Old Testament canon was the outcome of the *same kind* of confessional activity as the later reception of the canon in church (and synagogue). Once the notion of 'canon' is pushed back before the point at which Christian churches brought their canons into being, it loses its historical character. The continuity between formation and reception of canon is a theological, not a historical one, basically equivalent to the theological claim that the church is the 'New Israel' and therefore historically continuous with the old one. Childs is again apparently offering a non-confessional, historical way of describing 'canon' but actually selling a confessional one. If one could assert the historical continuity of the writers of the books of the Old Testament and their Christian readers, then a single discourse on the 'Old Testament' that was both historical and confessional might be possible. But the connection between the hypothetical producing community and the historical receiving ones is not historical.

For while the premise that the 'Old Testament' is a scripture/a canon is indeed a matter of fact (more or less: a student of any or no religion will affirm that it is at least part of a canon), the subsequent claim that the 'Old Testament' was produced by a believing community is more tricky. It has the outward form of a historical statement but is not. This hypothetical believing community (or communities) would not *historically* have believed what Childs or any Christian community believes. Indeed, its authors would not have believed much of what modern Jews believe. Their beliefs (assuming for a moment that they are coherent and consistent) have been retrospectively harmonized and Christianized by the adoption of the Old Testament as Christian canon. The claim that the 'canonical' approach is appropriate to the nature of the material, rather than merely congruent with a Christian history of reception is a false one.

Can we draw from this analysis a conclusion about the kind of discourse that Childs finally adopts? It seems to me that what he has done is to move implicitly from an 'outsider' view of canon to an 'insider' view. From the historical point of view that he starts from, namely the production of the books of the Old Testament, the 'canon' developed in many different ways. Within Judaism it eventually resulted in Jewish bibles (Hebrew and Greek); within Christianity, a different and fluid collection of writings, supplemented by a collection of purely Christian compositions, resulted in the production of different Christian bibles, containing different Christian canons. If one stays in this historical mode of approach, one cannot speak of 'the canon' at all; one can only describe the process by which over at least fifteen centuries Jewish (or pre-Jewish) writings developed into the Protestant Old Testament, which is Childs's 'canon', or part of it. To jump from 'canons' to 'the canon' is to leap from one discourse to the other. 'Canons' are seen from the outside. 'The canon', however, is very much an insider's language, for it must refer to the particular one which the insider accepts.

The 'inside' and 'outside' perspectives correspond essentially to what anthropologists describe as 'emic' and 'etic'. First coined by Kenneth Pike,[18] 'emics' defines an 'internal' or 'empathetic' description of a society, adopting what is called the 'native point of view', using the categories of the culture being described; 'etics' refers to an external description, using the categories of the scientific observer. The distinction can usefully be applied to biblical histories, depending on whether the historian is using biblical categories of description or non-biblical ones.[19] But it can also be helpful in differentiating between two

18. K. Pike, 'Towards a Theory of the Structure of Human Behavior', in D. Hymes (ed.), *Language in Culture and Society* (New York: Harper & Row, 1964), pp. 154-61. Cf. also M. Harris, *Cultural Materialism: The Struggle for a Science of Culture* (New York: Vintage Books, 1979); T.N. Headland, K.L. Pike and M. Harris, *Emics and Etics: The Insider/Outside Debate* (Frontiers of Anthropology, 7; Newbury Park: Sage Publications, 1990).

19. Although I did not apply the terminology, this distinction underlies my treatment of 'biblical history' in *In Search of Ancient Israel* (JSOTSup, 148; repr.; Sheffield: Sheffield Academic Press, 1995).

ways of describing 'canon'. The statement that the Old Testament is canonical can generate two different discourses, 'emic' or 'etic', depending on whether you are within a community for which it is canonical or outside such a community.[20] In either case the literature being studied can be termed 'canonical', but the word 'canonical' has already acquired distinct senses and carries different implications for its study. The 'etic' version of biblical scholarship accepts that Jewish or Christian bibles contain a genre of collected literature we can call 'scripture', alongside the Qur'an or the Book of Mormon or the Gathas, and adopts a mode of description that can be applied equally to all of them, permitting comparison and contrast by a single set of criteria and permitting such comparison to throw light on individual instances. The 'emic' version is concerned with only one 'canon', which functions authoritatively and normatively, and whose own concepts and ideology form the basis for any discourse about it. The 'etic' view speaks of 'canons' 'bibles' and 'scriptures', the emic view of 'canon', 'Bible', and 'scripture'.

Accordingly, depending on whether you describe 'canon' etically or emically you enter one of two possible discourses and engage in one of two possible agendas for a 'canonical criticism'. From the emic perspective you can follow the path of Childs (though only if you are a Protestant Christian),[21] while the etic leads one to ask how various Christian and Jewish canons have developed and functioned within the respective communities. It can also treat with equal interest and importance the role of bibles outside the communities for whom they are functionally canonical.

My argument is not that an emic approach such as Childs adopts is in principle uncritical or unacademic but that he appears to be supporting it with features of etic discourse and indeed, perhaps, also misrepresenting it as one. Thus, he is in effect accusing a certain kind of biblical criticism for not being emic, and apparently suggesting that from an etic point of

20. On the application of this anthropological terminology to biblical studies, see M.G. Brett, 'Four or Five Things to Do with Texts', in Clines *et al.* (eds.) *The Bible in Three Dimensions*, pp. 357-77, and in his *Biblical Criticism in Crisis?*, pp. 15-18. Brett argues that in fact Childs is not practising an 'emic' approach, though he and his followers often represent themselves as doing so (p. 18).

21. For J.A. Sanders's method of canon criticism, see his *From Sacred Text to Sacred Story* (Philadelphia: Fortress Press, 1987). It is important not to extend my analysis of Childs to Sanders, for whom the historical dimensions of canon formation are important.

view one can validate an emic one. The appeal, but also the danger, of the 'canonical' approach is precisely that it may present itself as valid both emically and etically, and give the impression of a single discourse. That is why it has been important to show that Childs is neither logical in his argumentation nor historical in his method. His popular approach has flourished among advocates of 'scripture' but ought to be strongly resisted by anyone claiming to practise 'biblical studies'.

*Postmodernist Issues*

Childs does not take in the 'newer' literary approaches, which have spread to the forefront of biblical studies in recent decades, and which also offer an alternative to his 'canon-centred' approach. It is these approaches which have often, like Childs, criticized historical-critical approaches for ignoring the main questions of biblical texts, which (they claim) is what the texts *mean*; and meaning is not dealt with by explaining how the texts came to be the way they are. But such literary approaches (specifically deconstruction and reader response) are often identified as the most inimical to theological biblical studies, because they are based on the view that language is unstable, and therefore meaning is to some extent indeterminate. The role, and the freedom, of the reader to generate meaning is highlighted at the expense of the author of the text, the text itself, and the text's own history of reception. Thus, the approach implies, biblical texts do not constantly and reliably 'refer' to something objective 'out there', including God, truth, the gospel, eternal life, and so on, but can only project characters, notions and 'narrative worlds'. They cannot represent a 'reality' beyond themselves. This philosophy of language offers both a promise and a threat to 'scripture': on the one hand, by insisting on the reader as the locus of meaning, it *can* be used to support a notion that the 'true' meaning of 'the Bible' is granted to Christians by faith or by the inspiration of the Holy Spirit, or it can help to buttress confessional readings against attacks of being 'subjective' by dismantling the notion of objectivity. On the other hand, however, it represents a challenge to a theology based on an objective reality to which the scriptures truthfully refer, by denying that any direct revelation of such realities can be mediated in a written text.

Francis Watson's ambitious book[22] is an attempt to define not only a place for theology in biblical study but a privileged and normative place. He is aware that there is a competing discourse (an 'academic', or 'non-

22. See n. 2 above.

confessing' one) which he regards as inimical to theology, and which, although he wants to deprivilege it, he also wants to place in the service of theology.

Although Watson opens by attacking historical-critical methods of biblical criticism and insisting on the 'final form', we can ignore these, because like Childs he is not prepared to discuss what 'final form' he is appealing to or why. In refusing even to attack historical critics on their own ground (as Childs at least pretended to do) he offers no useful critique. The main thesis of his book, or at least the most significant for present purposes, is about referentiality; the biblical texts, he wants to assert, point beyond themselves to the reality that is the triune God.[23] In the course of pursuing this conclusion Watson says a great deal about the claims that theology has over against a non-theological discourse. His book seeks to counter a range of broadly 'literary' criticisms but also attempts to reassert a theological hegemony over biblical interpre-tation,[24] attacking views of language that make it self-referential and that therefore authorize a range of equally relative interpretations, and even attacking the notion that what I would call 'etic' discourses are valid. In many ways the book is hard to understand, because of this double agenda. The attempt to construct a programme for a theological biblical study (what I have called 'scripture') is interesting, But for some reason Watson also feels obliged to demonstrate that (Christian) theology has a claim, over non-theological approaches, to a kind of normativity, and even, as I read him, to truth itself. He wishes to reassert a view of language that enables it to point to transcendent realities beyond itself. Since it is hard to disentangle the various strands of Watson's argument, I shall leave them intertwined, and hope that the reader can nevertheless follow me through the discussion.

First of all, it seems pretty clear that Watson is working with an 'emic' discourse. But one of the several confusions in his book is that he sometimes appears to accept the 'emic/etic' distinction and sometimes to deny it. Here, for instance, he is being thoroughly 'emic':

> *In its ecclesial sense*, the term 'world' refers to the vast social space that surrounds and encompasses the church, within which it is to fulfil its

23. *Text, Church and World*, pp. 241-64.

24. *Text, Church and World*, p. vii: 'The position developed in this book is, in a sense, a familiar one: that biblical interpretation should concern itself primarily with the theological issue raised by the biblical texts within our contemporary ecclesial, cultural and socio-political contexts'.

mission…In correlating text, church and world, the term 'world' must be understood theologically.[25]

The ground on which the debate is to be held is thus the church's own world-view—or at least the one that Watson wants it to have (which is not necessarily the same thing, but theology often prefers prescription to description). Watson is nevertheless also aware of a possible conflict of discourse where, as he puts it, the church and the university collide. But how does he represent this non-theological discourse of the academy (which we might provisionally regard as the discourse of 'biblical studies'), and how does he suggest that it should relate, if at all, to theological discourse ('scripture')? A number of lines of argument are opened.

### Truth and Faith

Following the order of his own treatment, let us start with issues of 'faith' and 'truth'. Watson cites the well-known essay in which Christopher Evans compared 'confessional' with 'academic' commit-ments, and thus articulated in slightly different terms the 'emic'/'etic' distinction.[26] But then Watson goes on, not to quarrel with Evans's claim that academic study should not result in proclamation, but to suggest that Evans is characterizing the church as being opposed to the 'quest for truth': 'advocates of academic secularity presuppose that the various disciplines that comprise the modern university are all engaged in the same quest for a single truth'.[27] The aim of this reply is presum-ably to deny the equation of secularity with truth and of theology with dogma, thus making way for 'theological truth' as one more eligible pursuit for a university.

But this line of argument does not answer Evans's point about confessional and non-confessional disciplines. The issue is not at all about *multiple truths*, but about the ways in which 'truth' is construed; whether, for instance, it is something to be sought or something already possessed; whether it can best be seen from the inside by a committed member of the confessing group, or is approached by means of debate and from the 'outside' by anyone else. The issue is one that does not divide most academic disciplines, but does distinguish them from certain

25. *Text, Church and World*, pp. 7, 9. My italics.
26. C.F. Evans, *Explorations in Theology 2* (London: SCM Press, 1987), pp. 69-83. Cf. also his *'Is Holy Scripture Christian?'* (n. 3 above).
27. *Text, Church and World*, p. 7.

kinds of theology: whether a particular discourse is appropriate for those who *are* searching for truth or belongs only to those who have found it, whatever it is. For there are discourses which are conducted in such a way that their premises are able to be challenged from within the discourse itself, and there are those which only examine the implications of a set of dogmatically derived and incontestable presuppositions. We shall see presently that this is precisely how Watson himself distinguishes theology from 'academic' disciplines!

Watson also fails to make clear whether he is content with a situation in which within the academy the proclamation of all theological truths is acceptable, or only the Christian one. This, of course, gets to the heart of the emic/etic distinction. An academic discourse that privileges any theological claims will quickly self-destruct. If all theological discourse is an examination (not a search) of the truth it accepts *a priori*, then the theological discourses of Judaism, Islam and Christianity (not to mention other religions) are unable to mix. This is precisely what makes emic discourses problematic: the insider view is automatically privileged and comparison between different systems becomes impossible. It is, we may say, tending towards solipsism. I take Evans to be saying that proclamation is inappropriate in an academic setting not just because the search for truth, which is the function of the university, ought not to be short-circuited or foreclosed by the propagation of dogmas that are held as *the* truth, but because academic discourse, being etic, permits various theologies to converse with one another. Indeed, one *can* do a useful kind of theology within an etic discourse quite easily—one which enables truth claims among different systems to be examined and compared, influences and common traits sought, and so on. But this is emphatically not what Watson means or wants by 'theology'; he wants a Christian theology which not only relegates non-theological discourse but by so doing cuts out any conversation with non-Christian theology.

Another way of misrepresenting the difference between etic and emic discourse is to introduce the term 'faith', and this too Watson does. He writes that 'the assumption that faith is incompatible with proper academic standards or with openness to alternative viewpoints is ultimately a mere prejudice, whatever the practical grounds for caution over this issue'.[28] Leaving aside the 'caution' and 'practical grounds' (about which I would like to hear more), we must see that we are again being led away from the real issue, which is not about faith (Evans, after all,

28. *Text, Church and World*, p. 9.

was a Christian believer). The issue is not about beliefs, but about their role in discourse: how far shared beliefs can be accepted as working assumptions, and how an unwillingness to share those beliefs exiles one from conversation. Should a critical discourse about the bible involve asserting the truth of the scriptures, or should it continually question that truth or indeed ponder 'what truth'? Whether or not one has 'faith' in them does not prevent one from seeing the difference between the two alternatives, nor indeed from practising either one or the other at any given time.

I find, then, that Watson is addressing what turns out to be an emic/etic issue, but trying to represent it in other, irrelevant terms. His invocation of 'truth' and 'faith' is especially curious, because in the climate of postmodernity which Watson is primarily addressing, there is no antagonism to either. Indeed, postmodernism itself is a celebration of emicism and in its extremer forms a denial of the possibility of eticism! But from Watson's perspective it would apparently be as unacceptable for Christian theology to have *a* place somewhere within 'biblical studies' as to have no place at all. His conviction of the objective referentiality of 'scripture' means that negotiation is impossible and thus (Christian) theology *must* monopolize biblical interpretation. This will become clearer in the next stage of the discussion

### Scripture

Among the targets of postmodern critics are (1) absolute claims to objective truth, (2) denial of the subjectivity of any reader and (3) claims of privileged discourse. Watson, however, wants *his* emic discourse (Christian theology) privileged. This brings us to the next stage of the argument, which is about the 'essence' of scripture. Watson commences his argument with the claim that 'the primary function of holy scripture is to be read publicly in the context of communal worship'.[29] It is possible that the reader may mistake this for a descriptive statement, and I am not sure whether this is what Watson intends. There is no evidence cited for it, and from what little I know of church practices, ancient and modern, much of the Bible is *not* read in public worship, and remains entirely unknown to most worshippers (among whom I count the majority of my own university students). Bible reading by Christians seems to me more commonly undertaken as *private* devotion and study. Since Watson's discourse is emic and his discipline is theology, I there-

29. *Text, Church and World*, p. 4.

fore propose to take it that he is *prescribing* what is the state of affairs seen from the theological point of view, which does not have to accord with how an outsider would observe it.

The claim of the church to primacy in biblical interpretation is next supported by another statement:

> 'Holy scripture' as a generic category is not an alien imposition upon texts whose essential being and meaning is to be found elsewhere, for texts do not give their essential being and meaning to be known apart from their reception.[30]

Here it is harder to see that Watson is making a theological prescription, for this reads more like a general theory of literature. But, again, no evidence, no argumentation, no citation of secondary literature are offered, and perhaps only within theology does this statement have to be true. From an outside perspective, of course, a different view would be obtained. The importance of reception history in the interpretation of texts is certainly recognized with increasing clarity in modern academic discourse; and biblical texts have undoubtedly come down to us modern Westerners in a canonical container.[31] But we are not, of course, dealing with a single process of reception, not even a single canonical form. Nor, if it were true, would an ancient corpus of texts ever be able to be reinterpreted! But there are more interesting features of this statement to be analysed. Consider the language of 'alien imposition'. Alien to *whom* or *what*? The various collected texts which are now found in the 'Old Testament' were not written by Christians, and to read them as such is in a sense 'alien'. (It is also alien to read them as 'Jewish', since rabbinic Judaism is also later than this literature.) Canonization is itself a form of alienation. Adding the 'New Testament' to the 'Old Testament' is also a very literal form of 'imposition'. Indeed, to read a two-thousand-year-old text (and usually in translation) is inevitably to impose an 'alien' meaning, which two thousand years of ecclesiastical tradition do nothing to ameliorate.

---

30. *Text, Church and World*, p. 4.

31. I like this formulation by Robin Lane Fox (*The Unauthorized Version: Truth and Fiction in the Bible* [London: Viking Press, 1991], p. 157): 'As for the canon, it is not so much like a padded room as a room with contents of different dates to which we have agreed not to add or take away. Do the contents therefore add up to a new whole, an interior with a style of its own? No doubt they do, but the objects in such a room do not lose their individual natures...'

Moreover, what does Watson mean by 'elsewhere'? This word reveals that he accepts there is a *non-*'alien' reading *somewhere*—perhaps the reading preserved by the church? Which readings might he have in mind? A church historian (or anyone familiar even with the *Cambridge History of the Bible*) will be aware of many 'church' readings, from Origen to Calvin, and find them all every bit as alien to the modern Christian as to the original writers of the texts. Or is *any* 'canonical' reading 'non-alien'?

Finally, what should we make of the phrase 'essential being and meaning'? Childs at least tried to argue that this 'essential meaning' was historically imparted by communities that wrote and transmitted 'scripture'. Watson is apparently content to assert that either the essence of the literature is correctly conveyed only by the collection of books as a whole (in which case each canon might have a different essential meaning) or that the fact of collection changes the meaning of the contents, which is rather a trite truism. In either case, one can see that the 'essential meaning' of a collection (however this might be defined) might well be different from the 'essential meaning' of any of its components. The 'essential meaning' of, say, Ecclesiastes can hardly be the same as the 'essential meaning' of Job or of Ruth; in some way does the 'essential meaning' of both become clear when they are put together in a single canon? What intrigues me about this statement of Watson's is that it might strike anyone familiar with theological discourse as plausible, whereas on the most superficial of interrogations it turns out to be nonsense.

The next step in our discussion is an explicit acknowledgment from Watson, in apparent contradiction to what he has been previously urging, that theological discourse is (as I am trying to argue) emic, and that there is an academic discourse that is not:

> It is true that non-believing perspectives on the text are a possibility and indeed a reality, for the academy does not normally impose doctrinal tests on those who teach and work within it. Such perspectives may have their own positive contribution to make to the self-critique of the Christian community, even if their readings of the text cannot be accepted as they stand. But precisely because the academy does not impose doctrinal tests, there can equally be no obligation to accept the myth of salvation through secularity and to read the biblical texts in the light of it.[32]

The implications of this statement for the possibility, and indeed the

---

32. *Text, Church and World*, p. 9.

ethics, of confessional discourse within the academy can be left for the moment. What the quotation clearly shows is that in Watson's view the confessing discourse, which, by inference, *is* subject to 'doctrinal tests', is useful only for '*self-critique*'. His emic discourse permits no possibility of being criticized from outside of itself (the word 'solipsism' suggests itself again). I suggested earlier that I was prepared to regard theology as a (conventionally, at least) academic subject. Watson makes it perfectly clear, however, that this concession should be withdrawn if his definition of theology is to prevail. Since his 'theology' is a confessional discipline, its academic, critical capacity is limited to exercises in self-regulation. It is a barren species of discourse, unable to cross-fertilize, and able to gain pleasure only from self-gratification.[33] But it is apparently *unable even to generate this self-critique without the help of the academy*! Self-critique has need of 'academic standards'! This posture looks a little hypocritical: it advocates the use of an acknowledged 'critical' discourse to serve the purposes of a confessing body, while rejecting any product of such discourse that does not meet the requirements of the confessing community.

This stage in Watson's argument raises an important question about the relationship between the discourses. Watson seems to be allowing that what he calls 'academic standards' have a place in theology; theologians should participate in 'academic' discourse, while subjecting its results to the requirements of theology. But is the position reversible? Should academic discourse (the one that imposes no doctrinal tests) inspect the confessional theological discourse from the outside without exposing itself to the internal values of that discipline? If not, the outcome can only be that the practice of 'academic standards' in biblical criticism will itself be influenced by theological concerns, and will then be unable to offer theology the 'academic' rigour that Watson says it needs. My impression is that this is precisely what *is* happening, and why the separation of the two disciplines is so important to each of them, but especially the non-confessional.

33. Watson makes this clear on p. 8: 'The interest of the Christian community in the theological disciplines pursued in the academy consists not only in the particular interests of empirical individuals [sic] but in a communal concern that current Christian discourse and praxis should be exposed to critical testing...' But if this statement is to be consistent with the earlier quotation from p. 9, this critical testing must itself be conducted by the 'Christian community'.

If the concern expressed on the front flap of Watson's book that 'biblical studies' wants to 'exclude theology from its concerns' is sincere, he need hardly feel wounded. He wants to give licence to theology to exploit the academic standards of a critical discipline but rejects its ethos and its conclusions when they do not suit the dogmatic prerequisites of his 'critical' discipline. It is surely not theologians who need to fear exclusion by biblical studies, but biblical studies that needs to fear theology!

*Referentiality*

Let me now return to what seems to me the crux of Watson's book, which is an argument (or an assertion) about the referentiality of biblical language. Here are two quotations from the closing pages:

> We here encounter the reality of the risen Christ, and the *koinōnia* of the Holy Spirit in textual form. Can we be satisfied with a purely textual reality, or must we assert an intratextual *realism*, that is, the irreducibly textual mediation of realities that nevertheless precede and transcend their textual embodiment?[34]
>
> The text refers us to the reality and the hope of new modes of human community, stemming from the life, death and resurrection of Jesus Christ and moving towards the eschatological perfecting of community.[35]

Note the phrases '*We* encounter', 'the *reality*', and 'Can *we* be satisfied with a purely textual reality?' It is important to pause over these banners of confessional language, because in gazing at them the issues that separate emic and etic, theology and non-theology, confession and non-confession are more eloquently expressed than any amount of explanation or even paraphrase. The difficulties that I, as a biblical scholar, have with these passages are considerable. Can I, as an academic, argue about these assertions? Am I free to question them? Watson and I can obviously both accept that for the writers of the New Testament the resurrection of Jesus Christ and the eschatological perfecting of community may be real. Expressed in this way the statement would embrace *both* of us in the same discourse, and keep us in the same community. But the language Watson uses has been chosen so as to include (some?) Christians and to exclude me, to drive home the wedge between church and academy, to show that the truth may be something that I still try to find instead of something I already know. The church, on this view, apparently functions to exclude the world from the text.

34. *Text, Church and World*, p. 287.
35. *Text, Church and World*, p. 292.

Watson, in setting himself up as a spokesman for Christian theology, has come close to confirming my tentative view that theology is largely an emic discourse, that it is only academic to a limited extent (self-critical, within the bounds of its own dogma), and that it speaks in such a way as to exclude many biblical scholars. None of this, I think, is true of non-confessional biblical studies, which may not allow the claims of theology to pass for truth, but do not require that their own dogmas are accepted without discussion and barred from criticism.

I am not sure that a truly academic theology is possible, but many theologians believe it is. As far as my argument is concerned, the kind of emic discipline advocated by Childs and, in a different way, by Watson cannot possibly be confused with an etic discipline like academic biblical studies. So why are both scholars trying to either absorb (Childs) or banish (Watson) the non-confessional discipline? I rest my case for the separation of the two, though there is more to be said by way of exploring the implications of this conclusion.

### Domain

I have been trying to show, with the help of both Childs and Watson (1) the juxtaposition of two different discourses within academic biblical scholarship; (2) that a different approach to 'canon' lies at the heart of the distinction between these discourses; (3) that 'confessional' discourse allows no legitimate place to non-confessional discourse, except (Watson) for the purpose of permitting self-critical scrutiny; and (4) that 'theology' has a vested interest in wearing a cloak of academic colours and thus in confusing the two discourses (in the case of Watson even suppressing the other). In the last analysis, too, the attempt to suborn one discourse in the service of another is not just confusing but unethical. It is time to look at the power relations between the different discourses, their respective social and political contexts, and their differing interests.

Each of the discourses about 'bible' has its domain. It is quite easy to recognize on the one hand the church and on the other the university as obvious domains of emic and etic discourses respectively. But, as I suggested earlier, while theology claims to speak for the church, it is not entirely clear how far churchpeople are aware that theologians claim to speak for them, or, if they do, that they really want this. There is, I think, a certain arrogance about some theologians in this regard. But the domains of the church and the *discipline of scripture* do overlap. Just as the discourses are confused, so are the domains to which they characteristically belong. Let us first consider books, and look at titles, marketing and readership. *Introduction to the Old Testament as Scripture*, though evidently addressed to a confessing community, is actually *marketed* to academic libraries and biblical scholars. No ordinary church member would be expected to have the necessary knowledge of the Bible or the history of its interpretation. A church minister might, but only if academically trained. Yet its audience can only be those who accept it as *their* scripture. The approach seeks to work *within that interpretative structure* which the biblical text has received from those who formed *and used it as sacred scripture'*[36](my italics). I possess this book, and shelve it alongside non-confessional books directed to biblical scholars. Yet the book addresses me as a member of a confessing community to which I do not belong, and do not *have* to belong in order to be a biblical scholar. Childs might seem to some readers to be addressing the entire constituency of biblical scholars, and urging them that his method is the proper one for everybody; certainly his book has been accepted as a mainstream contribution to biblical studies, and reviewed in all the major academic journals. Yet if it really is a mainstream academic book, and accepted as such, then I must wonder whether I have any business being a biblical scholar. I am certainly excluded *by* its discourse and *from* its discourse, because I am not a member of a church, and I do not recognize Childs's canon as my scriptures except in the cultural sense. Holy they are not, to me.

The same account can be given of Watson's book. His 'ecclesial world' is not the world I inhabit, nor the world non-Christians inhabit (and I doubt that all Christians inhabit his ecclesial world, either!) I am a biblical scholar whose interests are being either marginalized or excluded. But as I have remarked, Watson even excludes non-confessing theologians from his discourse, accepting that in order to do Christian theology you have to confess the contents of the scriptures. Although no theologian myself, I am prepared to accept, unlike Watson, that theology can be discoursed about non-confessionally, and therefore that theologians can converse in their own discourse with non-believers about their discipline. Indeed, I was taught Islamic theology at university by a non-Muslim, although, as I was aware, the primary locus for the interpretation of the Qur'an is the Islamic school. I was also taught Judaism, and the Jewish bible in Hebrew, by non-Jews, and do not feel that in order to practise biblical interpretation I should speak for the *yeshiva*. No Jewish

36. Childs, *Introduction to the OT as Scripture*, p. 73.

scholar I have met, incidentally, has ever complained to me that I am incapable of interpreting their bible as well as they do.

So the two books I have discussed are addressed to a confessing community, though they, and their publishers and university libraries, give the impression that either they are writing for scholars as a whole, and thus imply that biblical scholars who do not adopt confessing discourses do not matter, or that scholars who have a Christian faith *ought* to use confessional discourse.

Another area of overlap, between the domains of church and academy, is institutional. There are institutions like seminaries where the domain is often partly academic and partly ecclesiastical. They can award academic degrees, but often their employees are paid by a church denomination, their students headed for the ministry and picked accordingly. There is also an overlap within the individual scholar, who may be a member of both a university and a church, who owes allegiance to both domains (a majority, I would say). These individuals fall into different categories. Some feel virtually no conflict at all between confessional and non-confessional discourse, and can write about bibles without any sense that they are straying from one to the other—and who might, even after reflection, deny that there really are two different discourses about their bible. Others are aware of the difference between a non-confessional way of speaking about bibles which they professionally adopt in the classroom or seminar, and a confessional mode of discourse which they feel appropriate to church functions or to their private devotions, and they aim to keep the two distinct. Some, again, feel an ongoing tension, and are never entirely at ease with the contiguity and interpenetration of two discourses that they feel to be basically incompatible. I have not theorized these categories: I have both colleagues and friends in all three of them.

Yet another area of overlap of church and academy is in the public perception. Even in the opinion of many laypeople (I mean non-church and non-academic) the opposite is often assumed. In a recent local radio broadcast I was challenged with being an agnostic and asked how I justify working in a university department of biblical studies. A few years ago, a senior British politician (Kenneth Baker, then Secretary of State for Education) made a public remark (in the context of the issue of academic tenure) to the effect that professors of theology who lost their faith should hardly expect that they would be entitled to retain their jobs. The remark, off the cuff and ill-advised that it was, confirms the widespread impression that Christian belief is somehow a desired if not a required qualification for studying and teaching the bible.

John Barton was perhaps right, then, to suggest that many people (and not just Christians) feel that scholars of the bible working in universities ought to be there to help Christians understand their bible.[37] This means, I think, that many people do believe that a bible is the property of the church, and that while it is right for a bible to be studied in a university, such study is for the benefit of Christian believers. This view is understandable, if mistaken, and institutionally endorsed in many ways and many countries. Christian theology is taught as an academic subject in universities (in Germany it is even taught as either Catholic or Protestant). This is unproblematic if those who teach it are appointed on merit and ability, and if other theologies can equally well be taught on the same basis. But often religious affiliation is a prerequisite for teaching it at a university. In several countries of the Western world appointments to university posts in theology are made with the participation of the church. Church seminaries or theological colleges are often affiliated to universities; in Washington DC there is a Catholic University of America and in Dallas a Southern Methodist University (to name but two examples). It seems a reasonable conclusion to draw from all these factors that the university and the church appear to be entirely compatible institutions in the eyes of many individuals and societies, even societies where religions and state are formally separate, or where no other religion is, or would be, allowed such a privilege.

### The Importance of Non-confessional Biblical Studies

I imagine it has been clear for some time that while I have no quarrel with confessional, 'emic' bible study, or 'scripture', I do not think it ought to mix with a non-confessional academic discipline of biblical studies. My concern is driven not by any dislike of or opposition to Christianity or Judaism or religion generally. There are positive reasons for insisting that confessional interests should be kept separate. Let me begin by suggesting that confessional discourse belongs to a type of communication that in principle, in intent and in practice implies a set of beliefs that define a community between the discoursants, and at the same time reinforce barriers against outsiders. It can be said that all discourses to a degree inevitably operate in this way. Is not the discourse

---

37. See n. 5 above.

of the academy exclusive? Does it not shut out non-academicians, or
people who do have particular religious faiths? It is true that no
discourse is universal. But discourses are not all *designed* to exclude, and
some of them include more people than they exclude and do not
exclude in a very obvious way. It is also possible, I think, for a discourse
to be developed that *aims at inclusion* and not exclusion, even though I
doubt that the goal is achievable. The discourse of the academy is value-
laden too, and there will always be those who do not share its
humanistic, rational presuppositions. But I would resist the suggestion
that it is therefore of the same kind as confessional discourse, or that it is
merely a different kind of confessional discourse. It is different in
principle and intent from them. The main feature of this discourse is that
it permits and stimulates criticism of its own practices and beliefs. It
encourages the expression of any opinion or belief that is amenable to
public scrutiny, evaluation, contradiction or confirmation. It deals not in
truths but in hypotheses and paradigms, which can and do change as a
result of the discourse itself. (More precisely, hypotheses and paradigms
are the ways in which its 'truth' is expressed.) It excludes opinions and
theories and beliefs that cannot be challenged, tested, critiqued or that
insist on an absolute and non-negotiable truth. It excludes emic
discourses, but does not reject the expression of any belief or value
system that can be communicated and examined by outsiders, and thus
enables members of different confessing communities to communicate
on terms of equal privilege. All of these it does, and also fails to do; but
my allegiance is to a discourse that has these *aims*.

Let me suggest a simple analogy. Discourses are like currencies: they
may have an intrinsic value, but they are used mostly to permit the
exchange of goods between persons within a society and between
societies. A confessional currency has no intrinsic value, and is non-
exchangeable. It is a soft currency which is unable to be negotiated
outside its own country. A non-confessional discourse is a hard currency,
which can be traded between countries: it has an exchange value.

I want to draw attention to another distinction between the discourses,
namely the 'critical' factor. Where bibles are concerned, confessional
discourse is itself bound sympathetically to biblical discourse (which is
part of what is 'confessed'). Biblical values and representations of reality
can be modified, updated and bracketed out, but they cannot be resisted
or denied except on the basis of some other internal criteria. The
discourse is circumscribed. A non-confessing discourse about bibles

subjects them to evaluation from a range of perspectives, allowing the biblical literature to interact with different value systems and to have its own varied value systems compared and judged in what is analogous to a 'free market'. In other words, it is judged by criteria other than its own, and by values other than its own. This is how it is able to contribute to the process of 'interpretation'. The critical reader tries not to force her or his own expectations on the meaning of the text, is prepared to disagree, be shocked, and perplexed. In that way interaction of text (I might even say author) and reader is to some extent two way, or perceived as such by the reader. A confessional reading in principle denies the scriptural texts the possibility of behaving in a non-canonical manner, and thus, paradoxically, denies the authority of the text in favour of the authority of the reception-conscious and theologically informed reader. Such, at any rate, is the tendency.

It may be objected that a bible is *not* like any other literature. This is, of course, a confessional claim and could be disposed of as such into the discipline of 'scripture'. But the claim can also be considered within the discourse I am using. For a claim for uniqueness can only be substantiated by comparison on equal terms with other literature, other scriptures (if it is to be substantiated at all, and is not purely a matter of dogma). If a bible is judged by its own values, then its worth cannot be evaluated, since value only arises from the possibility of exchange. By the same token, any scripture could be said to be unique, every piece of writing, even. One cannot say whether a bible is superior, for example, to any other literature if it cannot be compared according to a common scale of values (I suppose this is what Watson means when he talks about the need for 'critical testing'). Claiming immunity for a bible, or insisting on a confessing stance as a condition of discourse simply removes Christian theology from an arena in which it can communicate (except by trying to impose its own discourse). Those who regard Christianity as a universal religion might even consider this to be a contradiction of that claim. For that reason, I would even suggest that an etic discourse is more an ally of the church than an emic one (if such is truly possible).

A non-confessional discourse of biblical studies affords access, by means of shared characteristics, to academic discourse generally, which is also characterized by being non-confessional: history, literature, linguistics, science, philosophy, psychology and so on. In this discourse the history of ancient Israel is a part of a greater ancient history of human civilization: the language of English bibles is the language of all English literature, the religious beliefs are part of the mosaic of human religious imagination and behaviour, the social laws part of the history of human social philosophy. Placing biblical studies squarely within a discourse in which several religions and culture are able to participate creates not a unity of truth or of value, but a universe of communication.

### How to Live with Two Disciplines

This book is an attempt to show that the difference between the two disciplines of biblical studies and scripture is fundamental, and requires conceiving basic elements in very different ways. What I do not want to imply is that 'scripture' is either superior or inferior to 'biblical studies'. Perhaps from the perspective of each the other is viewed as inferior in some way, but neither side has the right to a verdict on the other. I have stated my view that an etic discourse is proper to the academic domain, and have tried to explain why. But the academic domain has no intrinsic privilege of speaking about bibles over other ways. Emic discourses are a part of human existence. (There is, I think, even a kind of 'emic' discourse among academics, though ideally it should fulfil a social and not an intellectual function.) 'Insider'-language is important to the sustaining of human social identity. The language of worship, prayer, preaching, devotion, even sometimes of thinking, the language of lovers, of families, of supporters of the same sports team, even at times of women and of men—these are all forms of emic discourse, and, in an extended sense, they could also be called 'confessional'.

It would be inappropriate, nevertheless, if the non-confessional language of the academy were to invade church worship: the point of a church community is that it is bound by a common commitment which the language of worship aims to express, not to question. In any case, try paraphrasing the Lord's prayer into academic-speak! The discourse of a Christian community sustains a social view of reality, in which it worships an unseen god whose son has redeemed them from a world full of sin, who forgives their own sins, who responds to their prayers, and who will finally judge the world, and so on. While these beliefs can be described and analysed by etic discourse, the beliefs themselves are impermeable, and the reality to which they refer is largely immune to the kind of truth claims that etic discourse typically allows.[38]

38. In theory, no doubt, a document that proved Jesus not to have existed (what

Equally, though, there is a social world that the academy inhabits. And, like all social worlds, it is not the 'real' one, nor does it claim to be bigger or better. But it is a social world in which gods cannot walk unchallenged around the vocabulary, nor where private beliefs of an unarguable kind can operate as working hypotheses without constant challenge. While individual academics can have such beliefs (and not only religious beliefs belong to this category), the beliefs are no part of the social discourse and do not form part of the curriculum. The conflict is not about what you believe, but what you may be allowed to assume in your professional discourse.

'Scripture' aims at expressing the 'truth' of 'the Bible' coherently, and consolidating an understanding of the nature and function of scripture within a believing community. Little of this actually takes place within churches, but it surely sets the proper agenda for seminaries, who are part of the church domain. Yet what of individuals who belong to church and academy? I see no sound reason why individuals who work in a university in the week and go to church on Sunday or synagogue on Sabbath and conduct bible study in their church during the week should have trouble keeping their confessional discourse apart from the academic one in which the history of bibles is studied by a historical agenda, their language studied according to the methods of linguistics, and so on. A certain conflict within such persons is not uncommon, I am told, though not usually detrimental to either religious faith or critical competence. Indeed, if it is realized that the two discourses are in fact separate, and even operate with separate notions of 'truth', it becomes easier to accept that indulging in both implies no contradiction. Many believing scholars affirm things in church that they doubt or even deny in the classroom; but if in different discourses there are different concepts of truth, it is possible, for instance, to affirm emically the resurrection of Jesus Christ in church while denying that the body of Jesus of Nazareth revived and left its tomb. People who do this are not contradicting themselves, any more than chemists and physicists and mathematicians, who in their different disciplines describe what *they* would call the same reality in quite different (and sometimes implicitly contradictory) terms.

sort of document would it be?) or a philosophical argument that disproved the existence of any gods would end respectively Christianity as a religion or theology as a discipline. But it is hard to believe that practice would conform to theory.

Nevertheless, in practice there are those religiously committed persons who have an interest in confusing the discourses, not out of malice, but out of a belief that the discourse of Christianity needs to be critical, and that non-confessional discourse can lead one to the truth of the Christian religion. Rather than accept that 'truth' is a function of a discourse, they believe in one objective truth, which is that of Christianity, and accordingly any discourse must in the end address itself to that reality. But it is self-evident, surely, that such a demonstration can only be effective if the rules of etic discourse are rigidly applied, or else the etic discourse ceases to be etic and becomes incapable of providing any independent support.

Moreover, there is an ethical dimension to the coexistent of etic and emic discourses, which needs briefly to be considered; what are the rights and obligations of the respective domains that each discourse serves?

## The Ethical Dimension

The ethical dilemma entailed in the existence of two discourses and two domains is neatly described in the New Testament story of the question about taxes to Caesar.[39] Who pays for the discourse? Seminaries are sometimes aided by state funds in the form of student support, but often they are funded by churches. If the churches are paying, they can support what discourse they like. On the other hand, most university teachers of biblical studies are employed by the taxpayer. Even most churchgoers would, I think, agree that the taxpayer should not pay for church education, or for a discipline that only speaks to people with certain religious commitments. Indeed, many education institutions, including my own, specifically preclude discrimination in sex, race or religion. It would therefore be unethical or unprofessional to conduct a confessional discourse in Sheffield. It also goes without saying that one 'emic' discourse rules out another; religious 'believers' may have in common the fact that they have religious beliefs, but are divided by its content. They can only communicate where they happen to share a common content. Thus, even if Christian theology is not cut off from secular academic discourse, it is cut off from the theological discourse of other religions. The problem with emic discourses is just this: they cannot communicate with each other. That, I think, rules them out of universities.

39. Mk 12.13-17 and parr.

There is another ethical consideration, which is more personal. I for one am harmed by 'faithism'. I resent the idea that my study of the bible is not really relevant, proper, and that academic books can be written that explicitly exclude me. I do not want *anyone* to be excluded (as opposed to excluding themselves) from the type of discourse I practise as an academic. I hope I can write for Christians and non-Christians, and that we can agree about what the presuppositions and aims of our common (etic) discourse are. I do not require any kind of belief, except in the usefulness of universally agreed rules of evidence and argument so that we can genuinely seek to persuade or entertain each other.

How should individuals who are paid by the taxpayer but wish to speak for the church act? How do they serve both masters, God and Caesar? I have already dealt with the problem of reconciling discourses at the personal level; but there is the ethical dimension too. Civil (public) servants have to carry out the demands of governments and regimes even if their personal beliefs are strongly at variance with the government. Doctors or police officers whose personal commitments clash with the duties they have also encounter conflicts. Their professional ethics and their private ethics may collide. Many other citizens, too, have to live with a conflict of private beliefs that contradict public duties for which they are paid. If there is an unendurable conflict of interests, the usual recourse is resignation. Thus, if one insists on doing the church's work in the academy (or even vice-versa, though all churchgoers are potential taxpayers) then one is open to a charge of behaving unethically. In spending taxpayer's money doing research that advances churchly or Christian interests *and at the expense of the academy's interests* one is behaving unethically. At least, I make the suggestion.

But we must also not forget the student or reader. These, the beneficiaries, also have an ethical interest. The ordinand or ministerial candidate in a seminary requires to study 'the Bible' in such a way as to serve a Christian community, which is to be their vocation. These may wish to address questions that are not directly relevant to that agenda, such as whether there were two kings called Jehoram or whether Paul wrote the Pastoral Epistles (or when), as academic discourse sometimes deliberates. Whether they are obliged to depends on whether they or their church think this kind of question is relevant or helpful (and they might think hard about this!) More problematic is the case of those students who go to university to 'learn more about the Bible', by which they mean to inform and enrich their Christian faith. If confronted by a non-confessional agenda which refuses to take for granted that a bible is inevitably a Good Thing, tells us the truth about life, gives us the proper values and comes from God in some way—an agenda that refuses to provide a religious message for them—these students may feel they have been misled, and that their wishes are not being met and their expectations betrayed. It is true, after all, that without students who are religiously committed to 'the Bible', biblical studies would be a minority subject in a department either of literature or of ancient Near Eastern studies or of religious studies. Do those of us loyal to the academy want that? When it comes to our own livelihood, do we want to bother defending the integrity of our discourse?

The solution is clear—in theory! Such students can choose either the confessional discipline or the non-confessional one. They cannot have both, but their handicap is often that where biblical studies is concerned *they do not know the difference*. They believe that there is only one way to study a bible, and usually assume that this implies a prior religious commitment to it as 'scripture'. Given a discipline that makes no such assumption, they feel misled. Even non-confessing students in biblical studies classes are sometimes surprised when no religious message comes across. And so the choice has to be made clearer. When students are able to see the real issues that lie between a confessional and a non-confessional discipline, and what each offers to the heart and to the intellect, they can choose. I am not sure that the majority will necessarily go for the confessional. But I am not sure, either, that their pre-university education will make it clear to them that they can either study bibles or study scripture. My solution may remain theoretical.

## Whose Bible?

The aim of the remainder of this book is to offer some essays on biblical literature according to the etic discipline. This will not be unfamiliar to most scholars or students, because many other books have been written this way. But few have made their discourse explicit as I have sought to do. Readers and reviewers may initially react to this book as 'radical' or 'unsympathetic', or 'provocative' or 'sceptical'; or they might find that it simply says what they already know and like. The question I put to each reader is whether I have succeeded in being properly etic, remaining independent of the allure of the Bible's own rhetoric, the weight of its confessional reception history and the strands of confessional discourse which remain entangled in my discipline. If you ask yourself whether my interpretations are unorthodox or extreme, or even offensive, then ask by what canons you are making that judgment. What do I not like and why? Ask instead whether the arguments are well conducted, whether the ideas stimulate thought, whether the engagement gives enjoyment, and, of course, whether I clearly misread the written words. Doing this you are entering into the same discourse as myself. I am not trying to deflect criticism in advance: I expect many of my readings to be opposed and criticized—which is fine!

In the biblical story of Jacob and Esau, the two sons fought for the same birthright, and the younger prevailed by a trick, because the god and his mother wanted it that way. The brothers fought, then finally made up; but one still got the birthright. My choice of this allegory is actually inappropriate. I am actually trying to argue that birthright is irrelevant, that there is no *need* to struggle, that each brother, as was finally the case, can have his own land—and keep to it. The two disciplines are not contesting, and they do not have to try and blow the other off the map. There is a proper place for each, within society and within individuals.

But separate they must, or we shall go on fighting a needless battle about 'faith', 'science', 'academy' and 'church' which can only ensure that we shall never have any proper discipline of biblical study at all. And I have a personal and professional stake in resisting that.

Whose B/bible is it? It is yours—and mine. And theirs. It is especially for anyone who wants to argue about it with *anybody* else—and can use the discourse to do so.

Chapter 3

WHAT IS A BIBLE?

In the previous chapter, I used 'Bible', 'bibles', 'biblical studies', 'bible studies' and 'the Bible', and tried to make clear that the terminology is important. Thus, 'the Bible' is a confessional designation, 'biblical authors' an anachronism, and so on. In this chapter disputes about discourses are over and we are going to do 'biblical studies', not 'Scripture'. In this newly self-conscious discipline, as in any other, the first thing is to define the object of study. The objects of biblical studies are bibles themselves; not necessarily what their contents *mean* or how they were first written. Accordingly, the first question to be asked is 'what *is* a bible?' Note the lower case, since every respectable biblical scholar owns several different bibles. In a confessional discourse, the question means nothing, since 'the Bible' is already a 'given', and either one accepts one Bible only or one does not care much about the differ-ences.[1] In this chapter, then, and before engaging in any 'biblical interpretation' I want to answer this basic question in terms of bibles' historical and literary formation and their typical features. I am able to give only the briefest of sketches of what is a complicated and sometimes controversial subject, but the question cannot be bypassed, and in any case a thorough examination is unnecessary to make what is a fairly simple point.

1.   Those interested in comparing my treatment with a confessional one can consult J.W. Miller, *The Origins of the Bible* (New York; Paulist Press, 1994). It is subtitled *Rethinking Canon History*, and has a useful annotated bibliography of 'recent canonical studies' (pp. 220-43). On the other hand, John Barton's *What is the Bible* (London: SPCK, 1991), devotes a chapter (pp. 21-38) to 'The Book and the Books' which includes several of the points being made in this chapter. R.L. Fox, *The Unauthorized Version: Truth and Fiction in the Bible* (London: Viking Press, 1991) has a chapter 'From Scrolls to Books'; but despite its title, this is about canon, not the bible.

## What is a Bible? The Historical Answer

By the consent of common usage and reference, and as a matter of empirical observation, a bible is *a* book. But the Greek term for 'bible' was βιβλία 'books', not βιβλίον, 'book'. The same is true in the Latin *biblia*, as in the authorized Latin *biblia vulgata* and as preserved in the standard critical edition of the Hebrew (Masoretic) text, the *Biblia Hebraica Stuttgartensia* (these words are all plural). Modern English examples, however, have 'The Bible' or 'Holy Bible' on their cover (usually with the name of the particular 'version' as well). At some point in history, or more accurately, over a period of history, the word 'bible' came into existence, transformed into a singular noun. Yet we still talk equally of the 'books of the Bible' or the 'book of Isaiah', acknowledging that a bible is really not only a book but also a *collection* of books. The way the contents of bibles are commented on and interpreted, especially in academic discourse, generally respects the plurality more than the unity. There are very few readings of a bible as a single book,[2] and even one-volume biblical commentaries are commentaries on individual books bound in a single tome, and not continuous exegesis across the entire contents.[3]

The components of a bible, then, were not only written and copied first as individual scrolls but have more commonly been interpreted as such than as parts of a single book.[4] And yet it *is*, physically speaking, a single book, which is how libraries, booksellers and customers treat it. What makes of these *biblia* a *bible* is first and foremost the invention of the codex, a technological innovation that enabled many hitherto individual books (scrolls) to be bound as a single object (see below).

---

2.    An eminent exception is N. Frye, *The Great Code: The Bible and Literature* (Toronto: Academic Press of Canada, 1983). Cf. A. Wilder, *Jesus' Parables and the War of Myths: Essays on Imagination in the Scripture* (ed. J. Breech; Philadelphia: Fortress Press, 1982), pp. 43-70; Cf. also J.F.A. Sawyer, *From Moses to Patmos: New Perspectives in Old Testament Study* (London: SPCK, 1977).

3.    Where units larger than a single book are given a continuous treatment, this is usually not because of a canonical connection, but because of a hypothetically reconstructed original source, such as the Yahwist or the Deuteronomistic history.

4.    I have not overlooked biblical theology, which is not continuous commentary though it aims to embrace the entire contents of a bible in a single system. See the appendix to this chapter.

It is important to recognize, then, that the possibility of a bible is in the first instance a *technological* achievement. The presumption that many people have that its unity and singularity are somehow intrinsic, that its contents belong naturally together, is illusory, as we shall see. The earliest codices of Christian scripture contain different collections of writings; some of these collections we now call 'bibles', if we happen to think either that they contained all that their owner regarded as Christian scripture (and not just a part, as the very first codices did), or that they contain more or less what our own modern bibles do. But the earliest codices containing the range of Christian scriptures vary sufficiently to show that they did not simply transfer into one format a collection that, although physically separate, was already firmly fixed.

Thanks to the codex, scriptural 'books' ('scrolls') that were once independent artifacts (literary and physical) gradually ceased to exist, at least in any physical form, as individual works of literature, and were transmitted only as components of larger volumes in which they were now bound together ('bibles'). Thus, while it is now quite permissible to treat an entire bible from a literary point of view (see later) as a unified corpus, a single piece of literature, any kind of *historical* treatment must recognize a *process* in which collections of scrolls that were recopied into Christian codices finally resulted in 'bibles' with standardized contents—though, it must be added, *various* standardized contents, since Christian scriptures have never achieved a single definitive form. That is the reason why we need to speak of 'bibles' in the plural. To refer to '*the* Bible' is a convenient way of speaking but which is at the same time dangerously loose: it runs the risk of moving from empirical to ideal.

### Bible and Canon

It is also important to remember that 'canon' and 'bible' are not synonymous terms. Many textbooks and even monographs fall into the error of treating 'bible' as if it meant 'canon'.[5] A bible is a physical artifact, a canon is a list of contents. The canon is what a bible *contains*, although, as I shall mention later, I know of no bible that contains *only*

---

5.   The *Cambridge History of the Bible* (3 vols.; Cambridge: Cambridge University Press, 1963–70) aims at the kind of description being attempted in this chapter, but still deals at length with the pre-history of the contents and their interpretation; the discussion of the physical forms of bibles over the centuries is comparatively thin.

the canon. There has always been other matter as well. Yet when students or scholars speak of 'bible' they usually, or often, mean something more like 'canon': a 'biblical' book means a 'canonical' one. When they speak of the 'origins' or 'history' of 'the bible' they also usually mean the origin or history (or more commonly prehistory) of the canon. But while 'bible' and 'canon' *can* be used interchangeably much of the time without creating great confusion, as soon as we examine the history of bibles and canons we recognize that the terms must ultimately be kept distinct, for it is possible, as we shall see, to have a canon without a bible and vice versa. The former case was once true of Judaism and the latter (very probably) once true of Christianity. Let me explain this.

*Judaism: Canon without Bible*

The holy writings of the Jews were written, and remained until the Middle Ages, on individual scrolls (with smaller compositions sometimes written on a single roll, such as the Minor Prophets, counted by Jews as one book). However, over a period between the composition of the books and the Talmudic period (sixth century CE) the Jews, under the authority of the rabbinate, defined a body of writings. There was, at the latest by the first century CE, a recognized collection of five Jewish 'books of the law' or 'books of Moses', constituting a fixed number and order; other categories such as 'prophets' or 'writings' were referred to, but did not yet seem to constitute a fixed collection (we cannot identify from the Qumran scrolls any such thing as a 'canon').[6] The proper terminology for the literature we are dealing with at this period would be 'sacred writings' or 'holy books/scrolls'. The Latin-derived English word 'scripture' can be used only if it is remembered that in Hebrew, Aramaic or Greek there is no term which denotes 'scripture(s)' as distinct from 'writing(s)' or 'literature'. In the Qumran scrolls we generally find allusions to the sacred literature introduced by the simple formula 'it is written' or 'as it says' without explicit reference to a defined body of texts; in Sir. 24.23 the author refers to 'the scroll of the covenant of the most high God, the law which Moses commanded us'; in Dan. 9.2 the prophecy of Jeremiah is found 'in the scrolls', and in the New Testament we find the term 'the law and the prophets'. But there is as yet no Jewish bible, nor a Jewish 'canon'.

6.  See the very valuable discussion of this in J. Barton, *Oracles of God: Perceptions of Ancient Prophecy after the Exile* (London: Darton, Longman & Todd, 1986).

In the first century CE, both Josephus and the author of *4 Ezra* assert a fixed number of scrolls/books which constitute the sacred writings of the Jews,[7] though they disagree slightly on the number of sacred books that the Jews possess (twenty-two as against twenty-four). Both writers, in different ways, represent these books as inspired. Later still, the rabbis subsequently debated which scrolls 'defiled the hands' and which not, suggesting that they wanted to draw a clear line between some books and others. They also coined the term 'outside books'. So an agreed list of Jewish writings 'defiling the hands' was set some time after the first century CE (the so-called 'council of Jamnia' may be only a convenient fiction) and indeed from the first century CE onwards we can see a standard Hebrew *text* also being imposed on the wide variety of texts that the Qumran scrolls have demonstrated to us, as well as a series of Greek translations that follow this adopted Hebrew text.[8] The earlier Greek translation called the Septuagint is something of a curiosity. It is not a single translation of all the sacred literature. The 'letter of Aristeas' (from which the term 'Septuagint' derives because of the number of translators reputedly engaged in it) is probably a fiction, but in any case seems to refer only to a translation of the (five) books of the law. In fact we have no clear evidence of the date or provenience of other Greek translations now called the 'Septuagint'. The idea of a Jewish Greek 'canon' is dubious; the evidence of Philo of Alexandria is that the law was venerated, but his references to other books now in the Jewish scriptures is sparse. We are not on safe ground in speaking of a Jewish Greek 'canon' until we reach the second-century translations into Greek by Aquila, Symmachus and Theodotion of the books regarded as sacred in Hebrew.

From the ninth century, apparently, Jews began to put their scriptures into codices.[9] Among modern printed Hebrew bibles, the standard critical text, *Biblia Hebraica Stuttgartensia* (which is not a Jewish bible, but a critical edition of the books of the Jewish canon with some Masoretic annotations) is based on the eleventh-century *Codex Leningradensis*.

7.    Josephus, *Apion* 1.37-43; *4 Ezra* 14.45. *4 Ezra* refers to seventy esoteric books besides, which are apparently even more precious.

8.    See E. Tov, *Textual Criticism of the Hebrew Bible* (Minneapolis: Fortress Press, 1992); on the classification generally, pp. 114-17; for individual books, *passim.*

9.    The earliest Jewish scriptural codex known is the Cairo Codex, from the ninth century, containing only the Prophets. There is a tenth-century codex, also from Cairo, containing only the Pentateuch, and from this time also we find codices of the whole scriptures. See Tov, *Textual Criticism*, pp. 46-47.

Another critical edition, based on the Aleppo Codex from the tenth century is being prepared by the Hebrew University Bible Project.[10] Most other Jewish Hebrew bibles are based on the printed edition of Daniel Bomberg (1524/5), which itself is based on various mediaeval manuscripts, but also used chapter and verse divisions from the Vulgate alongside the traditional liturgical Jewish divisions.

The word 'bible' is a Christian term which Jews have now adopted. For this reason, there is no Hebrew or Jewish term corresponding to what Christians would call 'bible'. We find other terms: *torah*, which refers to the contents of the five books of Moses; *miqra'*, which means 'scripture'; and *tenakh*, which is an acronym of the three divisions of the Jewish scriptures.[11] One can nevertheless refer to the Jewish scriptures as a 'bible'. What is the correct terminology? Christian (and Jewish) scholars have coined the term 'Hebrew Bible', although the *tenakh* is not entirely in Hebrew, and of course translations into other languages exist.[12] The modern Jewish Publication Society English translation[13] bears the title *A New Translation of the Holy Scriptures*, although the word 'bible' is used to describe it in the Preface and on the back flap. I prefer the term 'Jewish bible'.

The main point of the preceding discussion is to explain that Jewish bibles are a more recent phenomenon than Christian ones, both in physical existence and in nomenclature. However, the Jewish 'canon' (the nomenclature and to some extent the concept is also Christian) is older than the Christian one. It should be remembered, however, that in Judaism as well as in Christianity, 'canon' does not imply fixed order. The imposition of a fixed order, though largely a matter of tradition and chronological or generic arrangement, is finally a result of printing.

*Christianity: Bible without Canon*
The birth of Christian bibles cannot predate the adoption of the codex form by Christians in preference to the more popular scroll (or roll)

10. To date only one volume has been published, M.H. Goshen-Gottstein, *The Hebrew University Bible, the Book of Isaiah, Vols I-II* (Jerusalem: Hebrew Bible Project 1975, 1981).

11. Torah, Nevi'im and Ketuvim: law, prophets, writings.

12. The term 'Hebrew Bible' would be appropriate if 'Greek Bible' were used as its counterpart. However, this Greek Bible would be Christian, including what we now call the 'New Testament'. Since 'Hebrew Bible' was coined to replace 'Old Testament' with what term should we replace 'New Testament'?

13. Philadelphia: Jewish Publication Society of America, 1962, 1978, 1982.

format.[14] If we are investigating the origin and history of Christian bibles, our chronological starting point is the time when the possibilities for a single book of scripture existed, and that is somewhere in the fourth century of our era. There are earlier codices of holy books, but not complete sets of Old and New Testament writings. The earliest New Testament manuscripts, for example,[15] which go back to the second century (e.g. 𝔓1, 𝔓5, 𝔓52) apparently contain only single books (though we cannot always be sure). By the third century we have papyri with more than one text, and the Chester Beatty papyrus 𝔓45 has four Gospels and Acts. None of these is a bible, nor even a New Testament, but the putting together of a chosen group of Gospels may well have had the effect of 'canonizing' that particular set, for we have no codices that contain the four canonical ones together with any others, though the order of these Gospels is not uniform.

Like most inventions, the codex improved. It seems at first to have been impossible or impracticable to have made a codex large enough to accommodate all the writings of modern Christian bibles. But from the fourth century at least codices of 1600 pages and more were made, large enough to accommodate all the scriptural writings; and hence it is from this time that we can speak properly of a 'bible'. Had a codex of this capacity proved impossible to produce, we would never have had bibles at all, but rather collections of gospels, letters and who knows what else? What would they have been called?

How did the codex, which has remained the form of book that we know today, come into being, and quickly emerge (which seems to have happened) as the format most popular with Christians The new format (as was noted when it is first recorded in the first century CE)[16] was to be of service to travellers and to libraries; it was both less bulky and allowed immediate access to the inner contents without the necessity of

---

14. See C.H. Roberts and T.C. Skeat, *The Birth of the Codex* (London: The British Academy, 1983). Much of what follows is documented there. See also Skeat's contribution 'Early Christian Book-Production: Papyri and Manuscripts', in *The Cambridge History of the Bible. II. The West from the Fathers to the Reformation* (Cambridge: Cambridge University Press, 1969), pp. 54-79; F.G. Kenyon, *The Story of the Bible* (London: John Murray, 1964); T.S. Pattie, *Manuscripts of the Bible* (London: The British Library, 1979).

15. In some of what follows I am indebted to Dr J.K. Elliott of the University of Leeds, whose seminar paper, 'Manuscripts, the Codex and the Canon' was delivered in Sheffield in March 1995 and will be published in *JSNT*.

16. Martial 1.2

unrolling.[17] Despite its convenience, the evidence is that the codex equalled the popularity of the scroll only in the late third century CE; yet Christian writings (not just what we now call 'scriptures') appear to form an exception to the rule, for they were already favoured by the codex well before 300 CE. It is not clear why Christian writings differed from the trend, though several possibilities have been suggested, including that they were largely used when the owner was travelling (e.g. on missionary work), or that they were regarded as 'informal' literature, where the codex was apparently less resented than in the case of formal literary works which, fashion dictated, should still be in the older scroll format.

Nevertheless, the earliest large codices that we could regard as 'bibles' come from the fourth–fifth century, namely those known as Alexandrinus and Sinaiticus, followed by Vaticanus.[18] (At about the same time the works of Virgil were also put into a single codex.) These codices share much in common, but they also differ slightly in content and a good deal in order (see Table 1 at the end of this chapter). They should correctly be described not as different version of 'the Bible' but as different bibles. They show that there was a widely agreed view about what scriptures were on the whole to be included in such books, but there is apparently no strict list, and a bible might contain writings that were not 'scriptures'. It does not follow that because it is included in a bible, Athanasius's letter to Marcellinus or Eusebius's summary of the Psalms are 'part of the canon' nor, indeed, that the inclusion of *1–2 Clement* or *Hermas* means that they were necessarily regarded as 'canonical', though *Hermas* is still found in the ninth-century Latin Codex Sangermanensis, while *1–2 Clement* are in the Coptic canon, together with the Apostolic Constitutions, after the book of Revelation. But we cannot be certain that a codex, even after the formation of a canon within a particular church, might not still include books that were not part of that canon. The creation of the idea of a 'canon', which seems to have be unrelated to the parallel Jewish development, except in

---

17. The earliest codices containing Christian scriptures were probably written on papyrus, though remains of such books are now only fragmentary, and they were gradually replaced, largely or wholly, by parchment codices.

18. According to T.S. Pattie (lecture at the University of Sheffield, 9 March 1995), at least two hundred sheep had to be killed to make the Codex Sinaiticus. This may help to explain the slowness with which the codex achieved its pre-eminence.

the contribution of Jerome when translating the Vulgate,[19] is not presupposed by the existence of bibles. On the other hand, the establishing of a canon may well presuppose the popularity of the codex format.[20] If so, the situation with respect to the Christian churches was the opposite of that in rabbinic Judaism: bible preceded canon. Whether this is something of an exaggeration or not, it remains a fact that the contents of Western bibles have continued to change, sometimes with and sometimes without a corresponding change of canon.

For no single Christian canon has ever reigned: the Catholic, Protestant, Ethiopic, Orthodox (Greek and Russian), Coptic and Syrian canons differ. The Ethiopic church has both a narrow and a wider canon. In many cases canons were, and are, a matter of uncertainty (the contents of the Vulgate were not settled until 1546). 'Canon', then, like 'bible', is a category of which there are several members. Whether a piece of writing is 'canonical' and whether it is in a bible is a matter of where and when you choose to ask. For the earliest stages in the development of both, 'biblical' is easier to define than 'canonical, of course, because we can consult an ancient bible and see immediately what was in it. And anything that was in it was obviously 'biblical': there is no other rational definition! Any book that has been included in a bible is, after all, a biblical book: that is a matter of fact and not for discussion. Whether the contents of the earliest bibles are 'canonical' is a different matter, involving an understanding of what the term might have meant at any particular time. (Canonical criticism, then, is not central to *biblical* studies but concerns a related topic.) Thus, for example, the New Testament of the Peshitta (dating from the fifth century) omits four of the Catholic epistles (2 and 3 John, Philemon, 2 Peter). The Ethiopic New Testament canon has 35 books. But no Ethiopic biblical manuscripts contain the whole New Testament...

The evidence of the variability of canons and bibles is most evident to Westerners in the case of the different Catholic and Protestant bibles.

---

19. Jerome's dismay in discovering that he could not translate several scriptural books from Hebrew into Latin is related to an issue that informed the notion of canon, namely authenticity and antiquity, but rather than presuppose a notion of canon, this issue is one that contributed to its formulation.

20. The Muratorian canon, once commonly dated to the second century, may be from the fourth: see A. Sundberg, 'Canon Muratori: A Fourth Century list', *HTR* 66 (1973), pp. 1-41; E. Ferguson, 'Canon Muratori: Date and Provenance', *Studia Patristica* 18 (1982), pp. 677-83.

The European Reformers changed the Western ('Catholic') canon by omitting those books which were not in the Jewish scriptures. There had, indeed, been dispute about certain books from the time of Jerome. But the official bible of the church (and unofficial ones, like translations, were prohibited until the sixteenth century) derived from the early Greek bibles, not the Jewish (Hebrew) scriptures. Extreme veneration for 'canon', which is currently so pervasive in confessional studies, is a rather recent development. Luther was not so respectful as to refrain from meddling with it, indeed from changing it permanently—though his own changes were tempered by his successors.[21] Even so, the 'Apocrypha' was not formally separated until the sixteenth century (the King James Version always printed it between the testaments), and not until the nineteenth century was it omitted from Protestant bibles. Now it is tending to come back into Protestant bibles! Since there are several ways in which the 'Greek' parts of the Old Testament can be incorporated in a 'Protestant' framework, quite a few different bibles are now available to customers. It is not difficult to understand why canon criticism tends to go along with a rejection of historical criticism, for historical methods can easily expose the variability through time of 'canon' and expose it as a fluctuating phenomenon, stable only if idealized and abstracted from the concrete realities.

### The Form of Modern Bibles

The issue of the canon in the fifteenth and sixteenth centuries had much to do with the emergence of humanism: Erasmus was a severe critic of several canonical books, and Luther, far from elevating bible over church, treated the canon with some disdain, regarding any book that did not 'preach Christ' as unworthy to be included. Bibles, however, were much affected by the appearance of vernacular translations and the invention of printing. The printing press made bibles into a mass product, and translation made this product consumable. But far from standardizing bibles (though it did help to fix the order of contents), printing has preserved and even enhanced their variety. After the codex it was the second great technological innovation to affect the development of bibles.

There are no modern bibles that include only a canon. Indeed, some contain an amalgamation of canons. My own copy of the New Revised

---

21. In Luther's printed New Testament the books he disliked (Hebrews, James, Jude and Revelation) are grouped at the end, in that order.

Standard Version, like virtually all Christian bibles in English, prints a translation from Hebrew where a Hebrew original exists and from Greek where it does not (with one exception). It has the same contents as a Jewish Bible for its Old Testament, but a different arrangement. Its *Daniel* is a translation of the Hebrew/Aramaic version of the book, with those parts included in the earliest Christian (Greek) version between the two testaments, as *three* different books (The Song of the Three Jews, Susanna, and Bel and the Dragon). Its Esther, however, is a translation of the Greek, though those parts additional to the Hebrew are marked.

The NRSV, then, is not merely a revised translation of the old RSV, politically corrected and so on. It is actually offering customers a different set of contents, a different selection of books. Some of what is 'biblical' in the NRSV was not biblical in the older RSV. This is understandably puzzling to many of my own undergraduate students, who often assume that they have 'the Bible' with them in class, only to discover that their or that their classmates' bibles are defective for the purposes of the class. The simple fact is that my NRSV does not contain anyone's canon, but is a mixture of Jewish, Catholic and Protestant ones. Canon is not bible; bible is not canon!

In any case, scriptures do not form the entire content of modern bibles any more than of the earliest ones. The extra non-scriptural material in bibles also various and can be little or much. As with all bibles since the Vulgate, the individual books are given titles, and divided into chapters and verses. My NRSV also has a list of contents, maps and charts, a cross-referencing system, a concordance, a preface, and an introduction to each book. These are part of *one* of the bibles I own. Most of the others (old RSV, *Jerusalem Bible*, King James Version, New International Version) have similar material, though no two are identical. They often have running heads (my NRSV does not) which tell me what is going on in the text, or what some editor thinks is going on. There are sometimes marginal notes to suggest alternative readings or to point to the original language. None of this stuff is any part of the 'canon', and while some of it represents a traditional component, my impression is that most of the added material in modern bibles is quite recent. The 'final form of the text' may be a theologically useful idea, but it can hardly apply to the range of modern English bibles. Modern translations may be either literal (Revised Version) or governed by 'dynamic equivalence' theory (*Good News Bible*), in which the aim is to try to reproduce the same impact in the target language as in the source language,[22] or they may be quite paraphrastic (J.B. Phillips's translation). There is also a *Reader's Digest Condensed Bible*, an *Amplified Bible*, and we ought not to overlook the famous *Cotton Patch Bible*. The final form of their bible has long been customized for different requirements of bible-reading Christians.[23] Calling these 'versions' or 'translations' is misleading, since there is no single object of which they are a version, nor single text from which they translate. They are, simply, different bibles. To illustrate this point, let us take one example of different bibles and how they render a parallel verse (1 Sam. 13.1):

*Masoretic text:*

בֶּן־שָׁנָה שָׁאוּל בְּמָלְכוֹ וּשְׁתֵּי שָׁנִים מָלַךְ עַל־יִשְׂרָאֵל

('Saul's age was one when he became king and he reigned two years over Israel')

*Septuagint: (1 Kgdms 13.1)*
This sentence is left out of most MSS. A few that have it give 'thirty' as Saul's age.

*King James Version*
'Saul reigned one year; and when he had reigned two years over Israel...'

*New Revised Standard Version*
'Saul was...[b] years old when he began to reign; and he reigned...and two[c] years over Israel'
(Note b states: 'The number is lacking in the Heb text...' and note c *'Two* is not the entire number; something has dropped out'.)

*New International Version*
'Saul was [thirty] years old when he became king, and he reigned over Israel [forty-] two years.'

It is possible that there are words missing in the Hebrew. But there is nothing wrong with the grammar or syntax of anything in the verse. This bible says Saul was a year old when he started and that he ruled for two years. The NRSV is incorrect to say that numbers are lacking. It should say that 'numbers may be lacking, or else the verse is hard to reconcile with other stories about Saul'. But at least it does not invent

---

22. See E.A. Nida and C.R. Taber, *The Theory and Practice of Translation* (Helps for Translators, 8; Leiden: Brill, 1969).

23. An excellent account of these and many other bibles will be found in A. Kubo and W.F. Specht, *So Many Versions? 20th Century English Versions of the Bible* (revised and enlarged edition; Grand Rapids: Zondervan, 1983). It lists 159 translations (part or whole) between 1900 and 1982.

figures. The NIV does invent them, making a guess at what number ought to be there (based partly on a guess in some LXX manuscripts, which is no defence). The KJV is the most interesting. It takes the Hebrew exactly as it stands, but takes the two years of his rule to run only as far as the action in the following verse, which is ingenious, if the less probable meaning literally.

What is the point of this illustration? Simply that modern bibles do things that go beyond rendering the canon into English. They add, explain and harmonize, not just through their ancillary material, designed to ensure that no reader misunderstands what they are supposed to read. But any reader who does not believe it when her bible says Saul became king at the age of one can read another bible instead. What is important for every reader of an English language bible to remember is that it should never be thought of as '*the* Bible'. If there is some authoritative, inspired, scripture that Christians possess, where is it? 'It' is, as far as the majority of churchgoers are concerned, legion. The 'Bible' of theology is not a real bible that anyone can touch, read or give the meaning of; it is some kind of Platonic ideal. As I understand the discipline, biblical studies is about real bibles, not ideal ones. These differing bibles are not to be called 'versions' or 'translations' either, as I said earlier. What are they versions or translations *of*? And how reliable are they as translations? They are prone, as the example shows, to massage the text of previous bibles to make something less problematic. In many instances the word 'mistranslation' would be better.[24]

A word might now be said about Jewish bibles. Over the centuries between the rabbinic period and the Middle Ages the scriptural scrolls were added to, in the form of vocalization and correction—the work of the so-called 'Masoretes'. A full Masoretic bible includes their

---

24. A fine example of the willingness of one modern bible to mistranslate its original is found in the NIV at Mt. 24.34: ἀμὴν λέγω ὑμῖν ὅτι οὐ μὴ παρέλθῃ ἡ γενεὰ αὕτη ἕως ἂν πάντα ταῦτα γένηται. The translation is given as 'I tell you the truth, this generation will certainly not pass away until all these things have happened', which seems unexceptionable; but a footnote reads 'The word "generation" (Gl. *genea*), although commonly used in Scripture of those living at one time, *could not here mean* those alive at the time of Christ, as none of "these things"—i.e. the worldwide preaching of the kingdom, the tribulation, the return of the Lord in visible glory, and the regathering of the elect—occurred then. The expression "this generation" here may mean that *the future generation*...will...see the return of the Lord' (my italics). My attention was drawn to this example by F. Zindler, *Dial an Atheist* (Austin; American Atheist Press, 1991), pp. 129-30.

voluminous apparatuses (the 'masora' proper), and even when omitted, their corrections and their punctuation, which often determine the exact sense, are included in every Hebrew bible and incorporated into every Jewish translation. The accentual marks which indicate the way the text is to be read out (or sung) are not translated. We can rightly speak of different Jewish bibles, then, though, unlike Christian bibles, the form of the scriptural text itself is consistent, apart from occasional variations stemming from different mediaeval traditions.[25] The best-known Jewish bible to many scholars is the *BHS*, the standard critical edition. Jews never use it in worship, nor do Christians. I know a few colleagues who take it to church to follow the lesson. But they do not, as far as I know, interrupt the lesson to offer a textual emendation. *BHS* is a non-liturgical bible, which is an interesting creature indeed. (Whether, with its critical apparatus, it is any use to final-form biblical theologians like Watson, I cannot guess.)

If, as a biblical scholar, I am concerned to explain the phenomenon of so many bibles, so many 'final forms' (which are of course anything but final!), I cannot escape historical-critical methods. Literary critics will be content to read whatever bible is in their hands, scripture scholars will minimize in some way the wonderful prolixity of bible production; only historians, perhaps are seriously interested in the basic question: 'what is a bible?'

To know why the various bibles that I own are the way they are, therefore, I need to know a lot of history. Bibles have a history because they are human artifacts, subject to the decision of humans: authors, church leaders, church councils, translators, publishers. Whatever bible you possess has been manufactured for you by a host of people who in differing ways have contributed to its format and contents. This process will continue; new bibles will come into existence, probably new canons as well (as the NRSV illustrates, and as the Church of Jesus Christ of Latter Day Saints has accomplished). Biblical studies ought to be concerned with what bibles are becoming in our own age as much, if not more, than about hypothetical societies, conjectured authors and religious beliefs of two thousand years ago. Bibles are not ancient texts. After all, before the fourth century of our era there were no bibles at all.

The problem with historical criticism is not what Childs, Watson and some literary critics claim. It is that historical critics (including myself) have expended their energies on examining the origins of the contents of

---

25. Tov, *Textual Criticism*, pp. 2-13 has a survey of these.

bibles, getting drawn into a debate in which theological agendas run free. The origins of the biblical literature, as anyone who follows scholarly and popular discussions will recognize, is a matter of intense interest because of the importance these questions hold for some people's religious beliefs. It is very easy for any historian to be drawn into a position in which he or she is 'defending' or 'attacking' 'the Bible'. By contrast, there is little religious interest in the history of actual bibles. But this is where the historical work needs to be done, where we have more evidence and where the cultural role of bibles in our societies can be more directly addressed.

### What is a Bible? The Literary Answer

Although it is perhaps the most important, history is not the only means by which one can answer the question 'what is a bible?' Confronted with any one bible, a legitimate literary approach to the question 'what is a bible?' can be generated. Every bible, after all, is a piece of literature between two covers, and is entitled to be read as a single work with a single meaning, if the reader desires to find or to create one. There is also the question of *use*, and bibles are meant to be read, either as a whole (which is rare) or in parts, or even piecemeal (which is the most common). In fact, bibles as a whole are rarely read even by professional literary critics. These prefer to read individual books, or stories, or groups of books. But here I am concerned with reading bibles, that is wholes.

An obvious way in which to read individual books is to construct the author of a text and try to reconfigure his or her meaning. But as a collection, the bible is not the product of any one time or place, nor of any one author or group of authors. A historical-critical reading of a bible can only lead one in the direction of atomism—the fault, not of the historical critic, but of the nature of a bible's contents. If one wants to read a bible *as a whole*, this kind of historical methodology needs to be displaced. But interest in reading a whole bible does not have to be confined to a purely individual and synchronic reading, for there is a historical dimension to this exercise too: one can apply holistic readings to creators and readers of historical bibles rather than to the authors of the text which bibles include.

Any bible will mean different things to different readers, of course, and modern literary theory foregrounds the reader in the act of creating meaning. But my interest in this chapter is in the shape and form of what is read, and so, begging the indulgence of competent literary critics, I will confine my remarks to the sense in which the *Gestalt* of various bibles turns them into different books and different stories; and although this section is about literature and not history, there remains a historical aspect to the subject of literary reading. Different bibles lend themselves more readily to certain kinds of readings.

The most obvious differences between Christian and Jewish bibles in this respect is, of course, the inclusion of the New Testament. Throughout the history of bible exegesis the 'Old Testament' parts of Christian bibles have been exploited typologically, although the historical has recently come to the fore. But the juxtaposition of two 'testaments' in a bible implies a reading strategy in which the New Testament provides the fulfilment, explanation or actuality of what is an antecedent figure, or provisional dispensation, in the Old.

But more specific ways of relating the two testaments depend on a Christian bible's particular format. It has been observed too commonly to need citation that the Christian bible opens with the beginning of history and ends with the end of history. Or that it begins with an earthly garden (Gen. 2) and ends with a heavenly city (Rev. 21). Indeed, there is a dramatic *inclusio* in the references to the river and the tree of life in Genesis 2 and Revelation 22. We cannot say whether this perception, either consciously or unconsciously, prompted the placing of the book of Revelation at the end of most early Christian codices, but the possibility cannot be dismissed.

Another obvious structural feature is the transition from the prophets to the Gospels. In the Christian bible the prophets are the foretellers of Christ. Specifically, Malachi ends the Old Testament (unless, like my NRSV, the Apocrypha gets in the way) with its prediction of the 'messenger' (ch. 3), explicitly taken up by the story of John the Baptist. Those early New Testament codices that begin with Mark tell this story more clearly, while those that begin with John tell the story of the Word of God that brought life and light again to a dark world (cf. Gen. 1). Of the early biblical codices, this scheme works only for Vaticanus, of course (see table), though since Sinaiticus ends with Job, this particular bible can have a rather different plot: the righteous sufferer redeemed and his lost family restored. If, like Alexandrinus, the Old Testament ends with books of Wisdom, the biblical story is one of Wisdom incarnated in the person of Jesus.

Reading a bible as a whole need not be chiastic: if the Old Testament is seen to be divided into law, history, wisdom and prophets, and the New Testament into Gospel, history (Acts), epistles and Revelation, further possibilities are open. Vaticanus has the order Law, History, Wisdom, Prophecy, Gospel, History, Epistle, Apocalypse: the two sets of genre can easily be matched.

Thus, given the freedom that every reader has to make a meaning from a bible, it is reasonable to suggest that the order and contents of some ancient bibles is affected by a literary reading of the entire contents. Perhaps I am suggesting that, within certain limits, each of the compilers of Sinaiticus, Alexandrinus and Vaticanus was constructing a literary and aesthetic 'canon'.[26] But of course alongside the holistic readings of ancient bible compilers stands the right of the modern bible reader to read holistically what is a single book. However, I would not be able to read the NRSV holistically in the same way as its predecessor, the RSV, because in that crucial gap between the Old and New Testaments lies a series of writings that need to be integrated into the overall sequence. (I have yet to do this to my own satisfaction.)

But what of the Jewish bible? Let us remember that there is little likelihood of a 'holistic' reading of a bible prior to its appearance in codex form. By that time there was no tradition of reading as one book. It was possible for Josephus, of course, to paraphrase the books in *historical* order, but almost certainly to do so he read what he regarded as the books of the prophets (everything except the Torah) in the order dictated by chronology and not following any 'canonical' order. The rabbis, too, read their scriptures holistically, but not according to any order. There was for them no 'before and after' in scripture. It was not read linearly, as a codex tended to encourage. Indeed, any student of rabbinic sermons can share their delight in weaving the most improbable texts together into a web of coherent argument. The unity of scripture was synchronic rather than diachronic, and canonical sequence features little if at all in rabbinic biblical interpretation. Torah was privileged, and read liturgically in an annual cycle; prophetic books were read in parts, together with some other texts, at festivals. But, as I argued earlier, until the Middle Ages 'Jewish bible' is anachronistic in fact and in concept.

The order of contents of Jewish bibles differs from all Christian bibles: Law is followed by Prophets (which include the historical books of Joshua–2 Kings, excluding Ruth) and then Writings (which include Ruth,

26. For this suggestion I am indebted to my colleague Meg Davies.

Lamentation, Daniel, Esther, Ezra, Nehemiah and Chronicles). The interesting thing is that there is no grouping of 'historical' books, as in
Christian bibles, perhaps reflecting simply a history of collection; perhaps
a conscious desire to de-emphasize history (along with eschatology) in
the rabbinic period, who knows? How do we explain Joshua to Malachi
as 'prophets'? Chronicles after Nehemiah? There are also variations in
the order of the last section, the Writings. Chronicles now appears last in
standard Jewish bibles, but in some codices it is first. Psalms, Job and
Proverbs vary in their sequence, as do the *megillot* (Ruth, Song of
Songs, Ecclesiastes, Lamentations, Esther). Most remarkably, some
manuscripts have these five appearing after each book of the Torah
(reflecting an ancient connection made by the *Midrash Rabbah*, a
rabbinic commentary on the law and *megillot*).

We can see certain principles at work in some biblical manuscript
sequences: from Genesis to Kings the order is chronological. Isaiah,
Jeremiah and Ezekiel are in chronological order (in terms of the assigned
dates of their eponyms). But this order is not found in every Jewish
bible. The five festival scrolls have a liturgical connection. But there is no
way of bringing these various principles to bear on a single process. The
final order of books in modern printed Jewish bibles is the result of a
combination of purpose, habit and accident. Unlike Christian bibles,
there is no room for suggesting that order could prompt different holistic
readings of *miqra*.

'Holistic' readings of the Jewish bible, then, are difficult if not
impossible to specify for individual Jewish codices. It is in this respect,
among others, that a crucial difference needs to be recognized between
'Jewish bibles' and 'Christian bibles': the former are relatively late and
did not create a mark on the development of Jewish attitudes to
scripture, already enshrined in liturgy and in halakhah and haggadah.[27] It
is legitimate, of course, now that there *are* Jewish bibles, for them to be
read holistically by anyone, Jew or otherwise. Indeed, many modern
literary critics who tend to holistic ways of reading are Jewish (I think of
Robert Alter and Meir Sternberg in particular).[28]

27. Although there are early Aramaic *translations* (of Job and Leviticus) attested
for the Second Temple period, and arguments in favour of Pentateuchal targums in
the rabbinic period. Targums are, in my view, mediaeval compositions. In any case,
their existence carries no implications for the existence or otherwise of a Jewish
'bible'.

28. Curiously, despite their sophistication, each has a tendency to ignore a simple

Let me now underline this last section. In the place of the confessional 'canonical criticism', a descriptive analysis of different bibles can in some cases suggest holistic motives in the organization of particular bibles. Something not unlike a 'canonical process' may thus be at work *in the production of individual bibles*. But the process is peculiar to each bible; there is no single underlying principle at work that determines the shape of the contents. Nowadays, as I have argued, reading a bible is more than reading 'the canon', or even 'a canon'. The basis for reading a bible as a whole is its existence as a single volume. But this volume exists in many forms. For this reason, no appeal can be made to any normative 'canonical' or 'final form'. There is every case for recommending readers to read books that they can buy. And bibles are what people can buy. They cannot buy, and cannot read, a canon. I hope that the forgoing discussion has made it clear that on the simple issue of 'what is a bible', confessional and non-confessional, theological and humanistic disciplines have to go quite different ways. Biblical studies should study bibles, and scripture can study scripture, if first it can come to terms with the fact that churchgoers will tend to think that 'scripture' is whatever bible they happen to be reading. And why not? History is on their side.

Table 1. *Contents of the Earliest Christian Codices*[29]

OLD TESTAMENT

| Vaticanus | Sinaiticus | Alexandrinus |
|---|---|---|
| ...Genesis | ...Genesis | Genesis |
| Exodus | | Exodus |
| Leviticus | | Leviticus |
| Numbers | ...Numbers... | Numbers |
| Deuteronomy | | Deuteronomy |
| Joshua | | Joshua |
| Judges | | Judges |
| Ruth | | Ruth |
| 1–4 Kings | | 1–4 Kings |

distinction between a declared or created *literary* unity and a presumed authorial unity. Or perhaps they are misread by Christian critics who do not understand what may be their rabbinic discourse. The rabbis believed in the unity of scripture, though obviously not in any fundamentalistic sense; they remained perfectly clear of the distinction between theology and history.

29. I am indebted to Dr J.K. Elliott for supplying the data in this table.

| Vaticanus | Sinaiticus | Alexandrinus |
|---|---|---|
| 1–2 Chronicles | ...1 Chronicles... | 1–2 Chronicles |
| 1–2 Esdras | ...2 Esdras | Hosea |
| Psalms... | Esther | Amos |
| Proverbs | Tobit | Micah |
| Ecclesiastes | Judith | Joel |
| Song of Solomon | 1–4 Maccabees | Obadiah |
| Job | Isaiah | Jonah |
| Wisdom | Jeremiah | Nahum |
| Sirach | Lamentations... | Habakkuk |
| Esther | Joel | Zephaniah |
| Judith | Obadiah | Haggai |
| Tobit | Jonah | Zechariah |
| Hosea | Nahum | Malachi |
| Amos | Habakkuk | Isaiah |
| Micah | Zephaniah | Jeremiah |
| Joel | Haggai | Baruch |
| Obadiah | Zechariah | Lamentations |
| Jonah | Malachi | Epistle of Jeremiah |
| Nahum | Psalms | Ezekiel |
| Habakkuk | Proverbs | Daniel |
| Zephaniah | Ecclesiastes | Esther |
| Haggai | Song of Solomon | Tobit |
| Zechariah | Wisdom | Judith |
| Malachi | Sirach | 1–2 Esdras |
| Isaiah | Job | 1–4 Maccabees |
| Jeremiah | | An epistle of Athanasius on the Psalter and a summary of the contents of the Psalms by Eusebius |
| | | Psalms (including 151) |
| Baruch | | Canticles taken from other parts of the scriptures |
| Lamentations | | Job |
| | | Proverbs |
| Epistle of Jeremiah | | Ecclesiastes |
| Ezekiel | | Song of Solomon |
| Daniel | | Wisdom |
| | | Sirach |

NEW TESTAMENT

| *Vaticanus* | *Sinaiticus* | *Alexandrinus* |
|---|---|---|
| Matthew | Matthew | ...Matthew |
| Mark | Mark | Mark |
| Luke | Luke | Luke |
| John | John | John |
| Acts | Romans | Acts |
| Romans | 1–2 Corinthians | James |
| 1–2 Corinthians | Galatians | 1–2 Peter |
| Galatians | Ephesians | 1–3 John |
| Ephesians | Philippians | Jude |
| Philippians | Colossians | Romans |
| Colossians | 1–2 Thessalonians | 1–2 Corinthians |
| 1–2 Thessalonians | Hebrews | Galatians |
|  | 1–2 Timothy | Ephesians |
| *The original order is rather* | Titus | Philippians |
| *uncertain from this point.* | Philemon | Colossians |
| *Hebrews 9 to the end,* | Acts | 1–2 Thessalonians |
| *the Pastorals and* | James | Hebrews |
| *Revelation were recopied* | 1–2 Peter | 1–2 Timothy |
| *in the 15th century.* | 1–3 John | Titus |
| *(Vaticanus had earlier been* | Jude | Philemon |
| *entirely recopied in the 10th* | Revelation | Revelation |
| *and 11th centuries)* | Epistle of Barnabas | 1–2 Clement... |
|  | Hermas... |  |

## *Appendix: What is Biblical Theology?*

One of the ways in which the discipline of scripture obliquely addresses the question 'what is a bible?' is by means of the curious genre of 'biblical theology', which attempts to restate the contents of 'the Bible' in theological terms, thus transforming the raw material of ancient literature into a product usable by systematic theologians, Christian ministers, or even ordinary Christians.

The genre[30] emerged from dogmatic theology in the seventeenth

30. The bibliography on this topic is immense. The fullest account is H.-J. Kraus, *Die biblische Theologie: Ihre Geschichte und Problematik* (Neukirchen–Vluyn:

century as an enterprise of collecting biblical proof texts[31] to support Reformed doctrine. The rise of Pietism and a heightened dependence on 'the (Protestant) Bible' led to a growing independence, and authority, to this 'biblical theology' in the face of ecclesiastical authority. Its separation from dogmatics thus became gradually clearer. With J.P. Gabler (who is often canonized as the founder of biblical theology) came the move towards an historically descriptive account, in which elements that were applicable to his time were distinguished from those that were not. Despite Gabler's own Christian beliefs, he recommended the removal of inspiration, authority and homogeneity from biblical theology and thus in principle initiated a non-confessional discourse. The introduction of a historical, evolutionary perspective led to the separation of Old and New Testament theologies, first apparent in the work of G.L. Bauer at the end of the eighteenth century. Modern commentators often review this procedure favourably, endorsing what they see as a process by which biblical theology became more critical, descriptive and academic. But it remained, of course, inevitably confessional, because the 'theology' was Christian—not that the practitioners were necessarily trying, for instance, to import Christian doctrines into the Old Testament; but the assumption was still that a theology of the Christian scriptures was valuable for Christian belief and practice. It served no obvious academic function. It was also (and still is) frequently confused with 'religion of ancient Israel', on the assumption that it was a reliable record of what Israelites *should* have done. This assumption was entirely uncritical.

The revival in the twentieth century of a reaction to the history-of-religions approach, represented by dialectical theology, has underscored the difficulty of separating systematic and historical modes of description as Gabler proposed. The nature of the enterprise is such that any complete separation is impossible. The danger, as canonical criticism also demonstrates, is that if history can be used to buttress theology, it

Neukirchener Verlag, 1970); D.L. Baker, *Two Testaments, One Bible* (Leicester: Lutterworth, 1976). For Old Testament theology see conveniently H. Graf Reventlow, *Problems of Old Testament Theology in the Twentieth Century* (London: SCM Press, 1985 [1982]), pp. 1-43 especially (and the bibliography on pp. 1-2); G. Hasel, *Old Testament Theology: Basic Issues in the Current Debate* (Grand Rapids: Eerdmans, 4th edn, 1991) also offers an excellent account of the origins of biblical, and then Old Testament theology, with an extensive bibliography; and still a useful account is R.C. Dentan's *Preface to Old Testament Theology* (New York: Seabury Press, 2nd edn, 1963 [1950]).

31. Hasel, *OT Theology*, pp. 11-12.

nevertheless cannot be dictated to by theology and so may well become an embarrassment. Can Christian theology allow itself to follow in the footsteps of the study of ancient Israelite religion? Since the efforts of von Rad and of the biblical theology movement in their different ways to find a way of reconciling history and Old Testament theology, the growing realization that this religion does not correspond to any 'biblical religion' puts the status of Old Testament theology in particular into question. Thus Rainer Albertz, for example (a former student of von Rad), has recently sought to establish that a history of Israelite religion is a 'more meaningful comprehensive Old Testament discipline' than Old Testament theology, because of its historical, concrete and comparative nature.[32] Here, yet again, we can see the issue of confessional and non-confessional discourse emerging in Albertz's suggestion that history of Israelite religion should *replace* Old Testament theology. The suggestion that one might replace the other implies some sort of common function and common space. In fact, Albertz seems to me to end up with a not dissimilar picture from that which some Old Testament theologians might develop. Studying a religion and studying bibles are different things completely, and to suggest that one should replace the other is curious. What should *not* be allowed, though, is that studying the Old Testament will of itself yield any insight into ancient Israelite religion, without the benefit of genuine historical research into ancient Palestine.

I doubt, in any case, whether 'Old Testament theology' or 'New Testament theology' can achieve the necessary blend of historical and systematic ingredients that such a discipline would require. Mere description of the views of the individual biblical writers does not yield a theology. On the other hand, any attempt to be systematic will involve value judgments about the differing statements in the biblical books about humanity, god(s), ethics, and so on. Description must yield to evaluation if any kind of systematic account is to be offered. Such a *systematic* enterprise can only serve the Christian religion. I would not *in theory* be able to rule out the possibility of an Islamic or humanistic or Marxist 'biblical theology', but what would such an enterprise serve? The 'Old Testament' is a Christian entity, and no amount of trying to be 'descriptive' will do anything other than deliver a confessional account of its contents.

32. R. Albertz, *A History of Israelite Religion in the Old Testament Period*. I. *From the Beginnings to the End of the Exile* (London: SCM Press, 1994); quote from p. 16.

Given that this genre continues to show signs of life, how does one judge which is a better and which a worse Old Testament theology? Many Old Testament theologies are taxonomic: one finds the category in which the largest amount of biblical material can be stored (e.g. Eichrodt: 'covenant'; von Rad: 'sacred traditions'; Preuss: 'election'), then, by dividing the drawer into compartments, one fits in everything possible. What doesn't fit has to be ignored or glossed. The winner is the one with the least left over and the neatest drawer. Or a 'middle' or 'centre' point (*Mitte*) is found and the contents arranged round it.[33] Or the New Testament is taken as the point of departure and the Old Testament orientated in some way towards it.[34] But having performed this operation, what is to be done with it? What has been shown? What learnt?

The function and purpose of 'Old Testament theology' puzzles me (New Testament theology puzzles me equally, but the New Testament is not my area of interest). It is easy to say what it is *not* and what it does *not* do. It is not a history of Israelite religion.[35] It is not the theology of any religion that ever existed historically. It is not Jewish theology, and without the New Testament it is not Christian theology either. (Biblical theology, dealing with an entire Christian bible could serve Christian theology, but hardly just part of it.) It is not a theology that any modern Christian is expected to adopt. What is the purpose of doing *and redoing* it?[36] As far as I can see it is a totally *academic* exercise (in the idiomatic as well as the literal sense) yet paradoxically one which, unlike biblical studies, or Christian theology, offers little or no scope for a non-confessional discourse.

33. Reventlow, *Problems of OT Theology*, pp. 125-33; Hasel, *OT Theology*, pp. 139-71.

34. Hasel, *OT Theology*, pp. 172-93.

35. This is explicitly rejected, for instance in H.D. Preuss, *Theologie des Alten Testaments*. I. *JHWHs erwählendes und verplichtendes Handeln* (Stuttgart: Kohlhammer, 1991). In his opening section, Preuss also agrees that the Old Testament does not *have* 'a theology' of its own.

36. Childs's revival of *biblical* theology responds not so much to a concern about these weaknesses, but about the over-historicization which initially led to the distinction between 'Old' and 'New' Testament theologies. But Childs's as a confessional discourse is not logically inconsistent. Another attempt to revive biblical theology is that of R.W.L. Moberly (see his 'The Nature of Christian Biblical Theology', in *From Eden to Golgotha: Essays in Biblical Theology* (Atlanta: Scholars Press, 1992), pp. 141-57.

What might correspond to 'biblical theology' in biblical studies is what
is contained in the succeeding pages of this book. These are studies of
the characterization of the deity, of the way in which the power of the
deity was invoked to explain and control economic inequality, of the
way in which what is seen as a history run wild is mythically presented
as the death of an old god and the birth of a new generation. These
studies are no more 'systematic' than were the authors of the literature
themselves. Nor do they commend themselves as correct, doctrinally or
otherwise. They are simply instances of the way in which texts that deal
with metaphysics, society, ethics and history in terms of myth, that is in
terms of stories about gods, can engage a reader whose own social
world finds no place for these myths (he has others). In his *Expository
Times* article, cited in Chapter 2,[37] John Barton suggested that some of
the best biblical interpretation was coming from non-believers. Perhaps
'reading against the grain' is more exciting. But we should remember
that the grain is not in the text but in the history of reception. Perhaps
modern reader and ancient author need to collaborate in finding some
better way to exchange ideas than 'biblical theology' can allow either to
do. Not being theologians and not being Christian is, after all, something
that modern agnostics and the authors of *miqra* have in common.

37. 'Should Old Testament Study be More Theological', pp. 443-48.

# Chapter 4

## WHO TO BELIEVE?

One obvious way (perhaps the only way) in which theological questions (i.e. questions about deities) should be explored in biblical studies (as opposed to scripture) is by examining the characterizations of deities throughout its contents. From an *etic* point of view, 'god/gods' can *only* be approached in such a way, that is as constructions within a publicly accessible communication. We can accept that, like virtually every other human being in the ancient Mediterranean world, each author whose work has found its way into a bible believed in deities, however few or many, and that they were telling stories or making conversation about categories of being that they believed in. But the only evidence we have about their private beliefs are their writings. Once we start making assumptions about what these beliefs *ought to have been* we have stopped doing anything academic, unless we are arguing from other evidence that we have. Questions about the religion of 'ancient Israel' for the most part find themselves going back to the biblical contents for their evidence; non-biblical evidence taken by itself tells a different story and suggests a more cautious approach to their writings.[1] An additional factor to take into account is that writers of stories especially are not obliged to express only what they believe: they are entitled to indulge their imaginations. What they write may be what they believed, but that does not have to be the case.

This chapter and the next are an attempt to tease out of a couple of early biblical narrative sections some perceptions of a deity (called Elohim or Yhwh or both). The assumption we can make is that the stories bear some relationship to beliefs and discourses about gods that writers and readers could share. They cannot, however, deliver a system of beliefs, a 'religion', nor a 'theology' beyond the confines of the

1. For a fuller treatment of this issue, I refer the reader to my *In Search of Ancient Israel*.

stories themselves, since stories create their own worlds. They certainly cannot be expected to deliver what those who adopted them into a canon wanted them to say either, or what we, whoever we are, want them to say. To be truthful, they cannot even precisely deliver what their authors want them to say, since these authors are being read centuries later, from defective texts and often in translation, by people who know too little of the cultural codes embedded in the texts. But that does not prevent us from reading, nor does it necessarily remove the sense that nearly all readers have of listening to another person. The construction, however fanciful, of an author behind a text controls the reader's expectations and verdicts. We may be resigned to misreading, but we like to think that we can have access to an author's mind. This is not a retreat into an old-fashioned view of reading; I do not pretend that we know anything very useful about the author beside what we conjure from the text.

Against the tendency of some biblical scholars to read biblical narratives in the light of an 'Israelite' religion (as idealized by Christians and Jews) a good deal of modern literary criticism has deliberately tried to read what is called 'against the text'. There are good reasons for doing this as part of a particular hermeneutical strategy. But I have no wish to adopt this as a conscious strategy. Indeed, my desire is to read *with* the text. What I want to read 'against' is a reading of the text already predetermined by assumptions about what the writers may or may not mean or should mean. These assumptions can arise from the premise that the writings are scripture and therefore must speak in consonance with the beliefs of those who venerate scripture. But the grain of the text must not be confused with the grain of its reception. Very often 'reading against the grain' is actually reading against the varnish, and may indeed be reading *with* the grain. While a direct confrontation between a modern reader and an ancient author is prohibited by all kinds of hermeneutical obstructions (including the fact that none of us can entirely read outside a tradition), there is surely a good argument for insisting that one should respect both the honesty of a modern reader and the intention of an ancient writer and deny any claim in the name of tradition or reception history or 'canon' to intervene in the task of imagining a direct confrontation between author and reader, which can take place, as far as that is possible, only when the identity and personality of the author are not prejudged but the author is allowed to be implied by the author's own words. As with the matter of the domains of university and church, I think this is ultimately an ethical question: the *rights* of authors and readers.

The book of Genesis, with which every bible opens, appears to tell the story of the beginning of the world twice. A similar sort of thing happens in the New Testament, which opens with four accounts of the life of Jesus. There are notable differences between the two cases: one is that in the Old Testament the accounts lie together in a single continuous narrative, not four distinct narratives, and another is that (in the view of most people) the four Gospels refer in some way to the extra-textual reality of a historical person;[2] the opening chapters of Genesis do not refer to any extra-textually encountered event. Thus the creation stories need not be compared and evaluated on the basis of some 'event': there is no 'tradition history' that putatively links the moment of creation to early accounts and on to the finished stories.

These two factors work in different ways toward the same end: harmonization. The birth of Jesus, whether or not we have any accurate account of it, can only have happened once and in one way, and the Gospels are popularly harmonized, for instance, in Christmas cards that show magi and shepherds together,[3] and recitals of the birth of Jesus that blend the census and the flight into Egypt, making of the two out of four Gospels that have birth accounts a single Christmas story. To keep the stories of Matthew and Luke separate would affect the celebration of Christmas as a memory of a historical event. New Testament scholarship, on the other hand, typically harmonizes the differences by means of redaction criticism, explaining the accounts in both Luke and Matthew as fulfilling theological and not historical functions.

The opening chapters of Genesis can likewise be treated popularly as a single account of the origin of the world. But scholarly reading has to face the fact that the producer of the book of Genesis apparently requires only one narrative line to be read. One can create the equivalent of different 'gospels' by identifying Yahwist and Priestly sources, but

2.    However, it is doubtful whether readers of Mark and John would be able to reconstruct the same historical profile from reading their two very different portraits. And almost certainly no gospel writer ever met Jesus of Nazareth. Perhaps the differences from Gen. 1–3 are not so great, after all.

3.    The separation exists liturgically, of course, in the later celebration of epiphany.

these are only hypothetical documents after all, and only explain the fact
of two stories, not their combination into a single narrative sequence.

At the second part of Gen. 2.4 the attentive reader of a bible suddenly
needs to find a reading strategy. The Jewish bible, which divides every
book except Psalms into paragraphs, indicates a major paragraph
division here, at the end of v. 3. But if readers happen to be using the
NRSV, they will be given more direct guidance: in the middle of Gen. 2.4
comes the subtitle 'Another Account of the Creation', though, since the
next subtitle comes at the beginning of ch. 3 ('The First Sin and its
Punishment') the reader will remain unclear as to whether what follows
resumes the first or the second creation account. The impression given is
that Gen. 2.4b-25 is the 'other account' and that thereafter the previous
account resumes. But it is quite obvious that ch. 3 continues ch. 2. So
the reader is being misguided, and, if intelligent enough, will continue to
be puzzled as to the narrative sequence.

Some kind of competence at dealing with recapitulated but differing
episodes is required by every intelligent bible reader, because there will
be other cases later on: after Genesis 10 will follow a different account of
the spread of the human race, and after the conquest of Canaan and the
death of Joshua in the book of Joshua, another attempted conquest will
begin in Judges, in which Joshua will die again (2.6-10). It may be that in
each case a different reading strategy will be needed, but the opening
chapters of Genesis are not an isolated case. It is almost as if the writer
*wants* the reader to sort out this kind of problem right at the beginning!

The problem is not necessarily a theological one, as it is often
represented. Contradictions in biblical stories are only a theological
problem if one has decided that they will be so, by insisting that these
stories should not contradict each other. This is a pseudo-problem,
whereas the true problem lies in the *nature* of the contradiction: it is
direct and blatant and beckons to the reader; it cannot be something that
has happened *despite* an author, nor even as the result of a 'careless
redactor'. It is a deliberate move, and the attentive reader cannot fail to
see here a challenge to her or his competence.

In the second part of Gen. 2.4 we encounter 'earth and sky' instead
of 'sky and earth' as at the beginning of the verse, and as right at the
start of the story (1.1). This inversion is coupled with a qualification in
the name of the deity: instead of Elohim ('god') we get 'Yhwh Elohim'
('The LORD God' as bibles conventionally render it). Then the very
prominent place accorded to the seven-day scheme in Genesis 1 is

abruptly undercut by a reference to '*the* day' on which the sky and earth were made. These contradictions are brutal because they are immediate and gratuitous. In each case they could have been avoided by saying the same thing in different words. Reversing the order of 'sky' and 'earth' makes no difference to the referential meaning; nor, presumably, does adding the name 'Yhwh' to 'Elohim',[4] while 'on the day', which in Hebrew often means 'at the time' or 'when', could have been replaced by synonymous expressions that did not use the word 'day'.[5] Such a cluster of linguistic contradictions is a kind of signal that what follows is to be read *against* what precedes, a clue that is reinforced when contradictions of substance, of referentiality, are encountered, where the order of creation, for example, is reversed, with humans first and animals last. Other contradictions can easily be found, but we can deal with them later.

Contradiction, of course, invites resolution, not necessarily by the removal of contradiction but by synthesis at some other level. Rather than approach a possible resolution by resorting to a philosophical toolbag and applying various methodological implements, I want to proceed by means of rereading again and again. Now, a first reaction to an account that seems to go out of its way to deny what has preceded might be to ask whether one has indeed properly read up to this point. Maybe we got it wrong as far back as ch. 1? So, having first come to the end of the story of the creation of humans (which for the moment can be as early as the end of ch. 3) we reread 1.1–2.4 more carefully, paying attention to the areas of contradiction. In doing this we begin to discover a rather broader area of interaction between the two episodes. This area embraces 'good'ness and humanity. 'Good'ness forms part of the refrain: after each creative event comes the quality control: it is all passed as 'good'. Finally, the entire creation is approved: 'And it was so.

---

4.    After ch. 3 the 'Elohim' is dropped. The compound is rare outside these two chapters, and may betray a concern not to lead the reader into the wrong kind of reading, in which two different deities might be supposed. It is also possible, though rather less likely, that this writer anticipated source criticism and wished to show that there was in fact *one* writer in control. The idea that a harmonizing redactor inserted 'Elohim' makes no sense; why not harmonize 'earth and sky' or rephrase 'on the day'—much more important cases?

5.    It could be argued that there is no conflict of referential meaning intended, and that one is invited to understand 'on the day' as 'at the time'. But the proximity of the two other contradictions and the provocative use of 'day', which is so prominent a word in ch. 1, makes this interpretation most unlikely.

And Elohim saw everything that he had made, and it was very good...Thus the heavens and the earth were finished' (1.30–2.1). The world is made good, everything in it is good. Evil does not have a place in it.

Now for humanity: in ch. 1 Elohim has tried every form of animal there is: flying, crawling, swimming. Each creature has its appointed domain: sky, water, land. Finally he has brought into being a form of creature whose domain will be the totality, which will rule over the entire world. The other creatures are constructed according to the requirements of their domain: with wings, or fins or the means to crawl. But the shape of the new creature[6] is not environmentally determined. This one is built for domination and rule. It is therefore quite appropriate that Elohim, dominator and ruler, should simply replicate his own shape.[7] The new species is the first to have a purpose of its own: (1) multiplying itself, (2) filling the world, (3) subduing it, and (4) having dominion over every living thing.

Humans are created, then, to occupy, fill, rule a world that is good. Yet this *raison d'être* of humans is immediately turned into a problem in Genesis 2 and 3, for here Yhwh places Adam (a *single* human) in a garden, which he is supposed to look after (this is hardly domination). And Adam is on his own. How on earth (literally) can this solitary human fulfil the tasks of reproducing, filling and subduing the whole world?

But he, and the woman, do get there in chs. 2 and 3, and onward. Genesis 2–3 narrates the overcoming of these obstacles so that the

6.   Only by reading Gen. 2 back into Gen. 1 do we arrive at the notion that Elohim created an androgynous being in 1.27. It seems much more likely from the context of that chapter that, as with the other creatures, the deity created a number of them, including both sexes.

7.   Wherever in biblical books there is a reference to the body of the deity, it has a human form, as do the great majority of heavenly beings. In Exod. 33.23 Moses can view Yhwh's backside, once Yhwh has taken his hand away from Moses' eyes; Ezekiel (ch. 1) has 'visions of Elohim' in which he sees a humanoid in a wheeled chair, surrounded by other beings with the 'appearance of the forms of humans' (אדם מראיהן דמות), and in Dan. 7 Daniel sees a figure (presumably humanoid, having a head, white hair and being able to sit) and another human figure (called 'the Humanoid', כבר אנש) who comes in or with clouds. Each heavenly being that comes to Daniel to interpret his visions also has the form of a human. In Revelation the heavenly beings are represented theriomorphically, but the deity sits on a throne and has a hand (e.g. 5.1).

purpose plotted in ch. 1 can be achieved. By the time we get to Noah and the flood, the two stories or episodes (I cannot decide which term is more appropriate) are in harness, more or less: humans have fulfilled the divine command, though they have become troublesome in doing so and Yhwh/Elohim has to start again. But how exactly are the barriers that Yhwh has placed in the way of Elohim's project overcome so that the project can be fulfilled? The means are a series of ingredients that Yhwh creates, perhaps specifically for the purpose. First, he plants a tree in the middle of the garden, whose fruit is forbidden. Yet Elohim had said (1.29) that the humans should have *every* plant for food. Now Adam will have everything that is in the garden *except the one in the middle* (not at the edge, where it would be less of a temptation and not so easy to get to).

The second ingredient, provided apparently as an afterthought, is a helper for the human, because it was 'not good that the human should be alone'. This is another contradiction to ch. 1: something in the world is, after all, not as Elohim had said it was (i.e. 'good'). But Elohim had created humans in two sexes in the first place—does this lessen the contradiction? At any rate, the role of the woman, whose creation 'makes good' for the male, and who will later decide in favour of 'knowledge of good and evil' plays a central role in bringing about the ultimate achievement of the aims of ch. 1. She is not created, however, for reproduction of the human species—at least *apparently* not so, at first.

The third agent is the snake, again created by Yhwh as the most clever of the animals and placed in the garden; an animal that knows something about the tree which the humans do not, and which, having the power of speech, it will inevitably at some point pass on to the other talking creatures in the garden.

The last ingredient is the prohibition itself, which furnishes the immediate function for all the ingredients together, plus Adam. Any competent reader of stories will know that prohibitions of this kind are introduced into a narrative in order to be contravened; otherwise no story! But sometimes the contravention is accidental. Here it is carefully planned, but by the same character that issued it.

For these deliberately introduced ingredients must line up in their semiotic square and deliver the object to the sender, fulfil the quest. The fruit of the tree existed to be eaten, and the command was issued in order to be broken. The snake and the woman have obviously been introduced into the story because they are *both* the 'helpers' (in the Greimasian sense that they aid the hero to complete the quest).[8] The naked (עֲרוּמִּים) humans will succumb to the clever (עָרוּם) snake and break the command. They will then 'become like gods, knowing good and evil' and be punished.

What is the punishment? The snake is subdued beneath the humans, the woman is subjected to her man by means of her sexual desire, and the humans are expelled from the garden. These 'punishments' match exactly the goals of Elohim: humans will have dominion over all the creatures (including the most intelligent, who now crawls in fear of the human heel), women will be subservient to men for the purposes of procreation, thus ensuring multiplication, and the humans, expelled from Eden, will inevitably end up occupying the earth. It is hard to accept that Genesis 1 and Genesis 2–3 are independent accounts that just happen to come to exactly the same end point. They are in some kind of collusion; either the author of one story is rewriting the other one, or we have a single author—and it makes little difference to the reading strategy. The contradictions and the resolution together point towards whatever reading strategy we have to adopt.

Those who read Genesis 2–3 apart from ch. 1 will be tempted to see in it a story of human disobedience and punishment, with humans in the wrong, humans the originators of sin, and humans condemned to lose primeval paradise. (This is basically the reading that undergirds the Christian myth of human depravation/deprivation and redemption.) However, reading Genesis 1 and Genesis 2 together shows that the disobedience and the punishment are actually *mechanisms for fulfilling the divine intentions in creating humans*. This does not mean that Yhwh does not blame the humans or punish them, but it does mean that, from his own point of view, the humans have fulfilled the purpose for which they were created by his alter ego, Elohim.

It is now time to return to the problem: how are chs. 1–3 to be read as a single narrative? Or as parts of a single narrative, even? My

8. For the semiotic square and actantial analysis referred to here, see A.J. Greimas, *Sémantique structurale: Recherche de méthode* (Paris: Larousse, 1966); for a brief account of Greimas and his followers in the context of biblical studies, see P.J. Milne, *Vladimir Propp and the Study of Structure in Hebrew Biblical Narrative* (Sheffield: Almond Press, 1988), pp. 49-62. An actantial analysis of Gen. 3–4 by David Jobling will be found in 'The Myth Semantics of Gn. 2.4b–3.24', *Semeia* 18 (1980), pp. 41-49.

suggested answer is in two parts. Chronologically, one must see the Eden story as fitting *within* the story of ch. 1. Within individual verses of Genesis 1 we have to fit narrative action from chs. 2 and 3. At the beginning is no earth, and at the end it is being filled by humans. Humans, made in the shape of the deity, are commanded to take the place of the deity on the earth and assume a status of domination and rule. This they achieve by becoming *like gods*, the better to carry out the role. Humans do not start out as a species of both sexes, but as one individual, then one pair, eventually becoming numerous outside the garden. We can see the Eden story as a kind of replay in more detail of Genesis 1, in which the impression of an orderly series of commands and consequent effects is shown on closer inspection to be a more complicated process altogether: humans were not exactly created as a species in one go; they were not made in the image of the deity entirely in one go, but they started off as one human, and while they had their godlike shape, they only acquired their godlike wisdom by disobedience.[9] The command they were given to go off and multiply and subdue was in fact the outcome of a ploy and was finally issued in the form of a punishment.

The second part of the answer is more involved.

## *What Did Eve Do to Help?*[10]

Readers will be aware that Eve has suffered a good deal over the centuries from prevailing interpretations, notably those in the New Testament:

> But I am afraid that as the serpent deceived Eve by his cunning, your thoughts will be led astray from a sincere and pure devotion to Christ.

> Let a woman learn in silence with all submissiveness. I permit no woman to teach or to have authority over men; she is to keep silent. For Adam was formed first, then Eve; and Adam was not deceived, but the woman was deceived and became a transgressor. Yet woman will be saved through

9. See J.F.A. Sawyer, 'The Image of God, the Wisdom of Serpents and the Knowledge of Good and Evil', in P. Morris and D. Sawyer (ed.), *A Walk in the Garden: Biblical, Iconographical and Literary Images of Eden* (JSOTSup, 136; Sheffield: JSOT Press, 1992), pp. 64-73.

10. With apologies to D.J.A. Clines (*What Does Eve Do to Help? and Other Readerly Questions to the Old Testament* [JSOTSup, 94; Sheffield: JSOT Press, 1990]), whose fascinating treatment is quite different from this one.

> bearing children, if she continues in faith and love and holiness, with
> modesty. ( 2 Cor. 11.3; 1 Tim. 2.11-15)

There is no need to protest unduly at the treatment of characters in
stories; if we prick them, they do not bleed. But since women have been
made to carry the consequences of one particular reading of the Eden
story, it may be helpful to underline the implication of the reading just
sketched out: woman was created to take the blame for male moral
cowardice and for male sexual desire. But, as the story makes very clear,
women are undoubtedly the bringers of wisdom and life.

For some reason, Yhwh intended that the function of humans, to
multiply and fill the earth, would be achieved by them in ignorance.
Instead of being directly commanded to do so, as in 1.28, they are (or
rather, the first one is) set in a garden to look after it, presumably to stay
there for ever. This creature is told not to eat from the 'tree of the
knowledge of good and evil' but the tree in question (which the narrator
teases us with: some scholars have even been obliged to assume there
were *two* trees) is placed in the middle of the garden, and the snake is
put there, with its knowledge of the secret of the tree, to tell the woman.
Once told, the woman has to make a choice, whether to obey the deity
or believe the snake. As it happens, she believes the snake, and not
unreasonably, since the clever creature indeed is telling the truth (3.22).[11]
But her decision is not the result of temptation or of her own weakness.
It is described as a free and rational decision. She saw that the tree was
'good for food', 'a delight to the eyes' and 'desirable for giving
discernment'. Was it the wrong decision? As I read the story, it cannot
be wrong, from the point of view of *any* character, including Yhwh,
since this deity has contrived it, and necessarily so, for without it the
plan for humans cannot be achieved. Yet Eve must bear the blame, must
be punished by the deity. She also gets blamed by the man (3.13),
though in turn she accuses the snake of a deception that obviously did
not take place. She is therefore not *all* victim: it was as wrong for her to
blame the snake as for her man to blame her. And perhaps, for the deity
to blame the humans.

In part, the punishment is, as we have realized, only a furthering of
the plan for humans: to expel them from the garden so that they can
multiply and fill the earth. But procreation is not, it seems, guaranteed to
occur naturally, as Genesis 1 would imply. To ensure that process, the

11. See D.R.G. Beattie, 'What is Genesis 2–3 about?', *ExpTim* 92 (1980),
pp. 8-10.

woman is endowed with a sexual appetite that will tie her to her man. Despite the pain of childbirth, this sexual desire (תְּשׁוּקָה) will ensure procreation. But the price will be female subjugation. And yet, unless matters were very different in ancient times (and there is no evidence for this) it is males who typically exhibit the greater sexual desire; in the books of the Jewish bible they are frequently satisfied only by more than one woman; they seek wives, not vice-versa, and they do not always stop with one or two. This is, curiously, the only part of this story that strikes the modern reader as counter-factual; everything else depicts the human condition (at least for the majority of the human race) plausibly: hard work, sweat, pain of childbirth, death, weeds, crawling snakes.[12] Does the narrator here betray his prejudice, perhaps, believing in the sexual appetite of women as a fact of life? It could not be, could it, that in this different culture that we cannot understand very well women *were* more sexually aggressive because they needed husbands and children?

The woman, then, takes the blame for fulfilling a divine plan of which she was ignorant—and carries the can for sexuality too. She is the victim of a male conspiracy between male deity, male author and, sometimes, male readers. Her exclusion from the worshipping congregation, her capacity for generating impurity, are all justified by her curse. But where does the narrator stand in all this? He (for I take him to be male) accepts, it seems, that the subordination of women is a fact, yet his story absolves her from the blame. The narrator, in his turn, seems to be putting the blame onto the deity, whose devious machinations the narrator makes clear enough, and which oblige humans to earn their moral autonomy at the expense of his curse. The narrator, *qua* narrator, exposes an unethical ploy while, as member of a patriarchal society, condoning its consequences. He therefore exhibits that divided conscience which is yet another component of the human condition.

The other aspect of Eve, and of women, is as bringers of wisdom and life. Enough has been written in recent years about women as the mysterious 'other', who possess the magic to bring forth human life but

---

12. The curse *may* read as if only men will toil working the ground. It is well known, though, that in agrarian societies women have to join in as well at times, if they are not regularly working this way. But since the curse on Adam mentions both eating and death, which must extend to women also, it may be that sweating and toiling are also intended to apply to both sexes, not just males.

also blood to explain the psychology. But I am interested here in a simple textual demonstration. Eve is called Eve (חוה) 'because she was the mother of all living' (3.20; the Hebrew letters also form the verb 'to live'). Without this first woman there would be no living humans, for this couple would have remained alive only by eating from the tree of life (see next verse, 3.22). That she herself comes from within the man (if that is the correct way to read the text)[13] may indicate a male response to the primacy of woman here. But let us be fair to the narrator: he acknowledges that women are the givers of life. To be equally fair to women, it is hardly something to be denied.

But women are also bringers of wisdom. It is Eve who brings the 'opening of the eyes' and the 'knowledge of good and evil' to the man (probably having acquired it first). I suspect we are intended to see her here both as mother, first instructor of the child, and as wife, provider of meals to her husband. The 'wise woman' walks the stage a few times in the Old Testament (2 Sam. 14.2; 20.16-22; Prov. 14.1) but perhaps not enough to establish her as a stock figure. More interesting is the female personification of wisdom in Prov. 8.22-36.

> Yhwh brought me forth (קנני) as the first of his project, before his deeds of old; I was appointed from eternity, from the beginning, before the world began. When there were no oceans, I was born, when there were no springs abounding with water; before the mountains were settled in place, before the hills, I was given birth, before he made the earth or its fields or any of the dust (פרות) of the world. I was there when he set the heavens in place, when he marked out the horizon on the face of the deep, when he established the clouds above and fixed securely the fountains of the deep, when he gave the sea its boundary so the waters would not overstep his command, and when he marked out the foundations of the earth. Then I was the craftsman at his side (אצלו אמן). I was filled with delight day by day, rejoicing always in his presence, rejoicing in his whole world and delighting in humanity. Now then, my children, listen to me; blessed are those who keep my ways. Listen to my instruction and be wise; do not ignore it. Blessed is whoever listens to me, watching daily at my doors, waiting at my doorway. For whoever finds me finds life and receives favour from Yhwh. But whoever fails to find me harms themselves; all who hate me love death.

---

13. I accept and agree that until the creation of Eve, Adam should logically be understood as androgynous or sexually neutral. But I suspect that the male readership of the text, and perhaps also the male author, either deliberately or unreflectively assumed Adam to be male. It is not an important issue for my reading.

The text is obviously an intertext to Genesis 1–3, by which I mean not that there is necessarily any conscious allusion either way, but that the two texts are capable, by means of their language and their reference, to assist in each other's reading. Here is a female figure, the personification of wisdom, born at the beginning of creation, always by Yhwh's side. There (in Gen. 2) is Adam's 'helper' through whom humanity receives life and wisdom, who is 'known' (Gen. 3.1) by her husband. In the light of this intertext, the figure of Eve as the partner of the deity, the agent of his plans, bringer of life and knowledge to humans, takes on a different shape. It is not fitting, says Proverbs 8, for Yhwh to be alone. He too needs a helper. But throughout the stories in the Jewish bible he is alone, a lone deity, a confirmed bachelor happier with the company of men. The consequence of Yhwh having used Eve is that he will never deal with women again, at least not in a regular way. For this reason 'a man will leave his father and mother and be united to his woman, and they will become one flesh' (Gen. 2.24). This text has attracted the attention of commentators either as an affirmation of the importance of (monogamous) marriage or as an indication of bygone matrilocal customs. Neither of these conditions is actually a norm in the writings of the Jewish bible.

Another approach to Gen. 2.24 takes its cue from Lk. 3.38, which names 'God' as the father of Adam. From the poor deity's point of view, his son departed from him (in terms of disobedience and then in leaving the family home, the garden) and took up with his woman. Such a bereavement would explain the desire of this same deity to adopt an entire nation as foster-children, favouring the males, referring to their disloyalty by using the metaphor of chasing after women, trying to secure obedience through a legal agreement and so on. But this line of interpretation is taking us rather too far from the immediate question.

After this detour, it is time to return once again to the problem of reading Genesis 1 and Genesis 2–3. A partial account has been offered, but there are contradictions still to be explained. What about the order of creation, and the time it took? Why are we human readers being given different answers? There is no way round assertions that are directly in conflict, unless we want to break up the narrative into sources or to force it to say what it does not say. We are left in the position of Eve, with two authoritative accounts that do not cohere. The story itself reeks with deceit, too. Humans cannot be trusted: the man blames the woman, the woman blames the snake. But neither can deities be trusted: Yhwh blames all of them. But, as in the case of Job, he keeps the humans in the dark as to his real motives. In the end the humans can only accept that they are to blame, and (here, at any rate) perhaps pass it on to someone else. Being human means deceiving and being deceived.

And why should human authors and readers be any different? Readers seem to want to find the foolproof. For some of us, biblical contents are foolproof, for others, biblical narrators.[14] Here, though, we are dealing with a rather clever narrator, who has teased us by his contradictions into reading his story with great care and attention. And he still has the last laugh, however, because in the end he shows himself to be unreliable. Neither you nor I, he says, know how or when or why the world was created. We only know how it is. And where does this leave the rest of his story? Like Eve, we are left to make our own judgment about whom to believe, and live with the consequences, whatever they are, for us as readers, and for the reliability of the narratives that follow. It is an excellent way to begin a bible, I think, setting readers, narrators and the deities they invoke in a game of deception, guessing and unavoidable decision making. The only thing the narrator forgot to tell us is that the tree of the knowledge of good and evil was made into paper...

---

14. The most famous exponent of 'foolproof' composition' is M. Sternberg, *The Poetics of Biblical Narrative: Ideological Literature and the Drama of Reading* (Bloomington: Indiana University Press, 1985). But see too the strong criticism of D.M. Gunn, 'Reading Right: Reliable and Omniscient Narrator, Omniscient God and Foolproof Composition', in Clines *et al.* (eds.), *The Bible in Three Dimensions*, pp. 53-64.

Chapter 5

MALE BONDING:
A TALE OF TWO BUDDIES*

And he [Abram] believed in Yhwh; and he reckoned it to him as
righteousness. And he said to him, 'I am Yhwh, who brought you out of
Ur of the Chaldeans, to give you this land as an inheritance'. And he said,
'Lord God, how shall I know that I am going to inherit it...?' (Gen.
15.6-8)

By the first century of our era, Abraham[1] was already being
presented as the ancestor of the Jews and as the prototypical Jew. To
any author retelling his story, Abraham was offered as the paradigm of
what that author regarded as quintessentially 'Jewish', be it the rejection
of idols and study of astrology (e.g. *Genesis Apocryphon, Apocalypse of
Abraham*), obedience to the law (e.g. *Jubilees*), expertise in astrology, or
intercession for all humanity (e.g. *Testament of Abraham*).[2] In the New
Testament (Rom. 4; Gal. 3.6-9; Heb. 11; Jas 2.21-24) it is his 'faith' that
is highlighted, this being the key by which he is adopted as specifically
the ancestor of believers in Christ. The characteristic most often
attributed to Abraham in current Christian interpretation is his obedience,
of which two examples shine out: his trek from Haran to another land,
and his near-sacrifice of Isaac; in each case his response to a divine
summons appears immediate and without question.[3]

\*    A version of this reading appeared in *Bible Review* 11 (1995), pp. 24-33,
44-45.
    1.    I shall use the fuller name 'Abraham' even when dealing with the part of the
biblical story where he is Abram.
    2.    A treatment of the figure of Abraham in the Judaism of the late Second
Temple period will be found in the dissertation of my erstwhile student Nancy L.
Calvert, 'Abraham Traditions in Middle Jewish Literature: Implications for the
Interpretation of Galatians and Romans' (PhD dissertation, University of Sheffield,
1993), pp. 26-294.
    3.    But see P.D. Miscall, *The Workings of Old Testament Narrative*

Without the benefit of this long history of interpretation, how would *we* read the story of Abraham? Since very few of us can pretend we know nothing about Abraham before we read his story, we must make an effort to resist seeing what we think we need to see. That requires very detailed attention to the text itself. The following is a reading that presumes nothing about the values of the author of the story (except that it was an ancient Judaean) and takes Abraham, his deity and his world to be projections of that author's creativity.

Where does the story of Abraham begin? Commentators frequently begin at Gen. 12.1, which contains the so-called 'call of Abram'. But in order to get in the whole story we need to start earlier. From Genesis 11 we learn that the god Yhwh (as I shall call him throughout, though he is sometimes referred to as Elohim) is currently spreading the nations over the earth, scattering them from their original base in Babylonia (Shinar). This activity is described as a deliberate divine resettlement policy, provoked by human ambition, because Yhwh is worried about what humans might do if they cooperate with each other.[4] Thus, Yhwh wants to keep the human race reasonably powerless and pacific, to prevent the mischief that can occur when people speak the same language and live in the same city. And so, in line with this redistribution of the earth's peoples, Terah and his family are allocated their plot of land, and so went from Ur of the Chaldeans 'to go to the land of Canaan' (11.31).[5]

We are reminded of this in 15.7 when Yhwh informs Abraham that he brought him from Ur of the Chaldeans (and not from Haran!) But the family stopped when they reached Haran, not temporarily, but to 'settle down' there (יָשַׁב). Why? We are given no answer, but the name of the city (חָרָן) is curiously similar to the name of Terah's eldest son (הָרָן). Haran had already died in Ur (11.28); perhaps Terah was struck by the similarity (the names are identical in conventional English transliteration)

---

(Philadelphia: Fortress Press; Chico, CA: Scholars Press, 1983), pp. 11-46, who shows how ambiguous the silence of Abraham is.

4.    This kind of population resettlement, incidentally, was what the Assyrians did to  peoples under their dominion, particularly in response to unacceptable political ambitions on the part of vassals: one of their victims was the kingdom of Israel, and their successors, the Babylonians, did the same to Judah. Yhwh's actions would therefore perhaps not seem so strange to ancient readers. But modern readers do not *need* to know this.

5.    For this idea, see T.L. Thompson, *The Origin Tradition of Ancient Israel* (JSOTSup, 55; Sheffield: JSOT Press, 1987), pp.79-80.

and stayed for sentimental reasons. Or we shall have to leave this decision unexplained.

The fact is, nevertheless, that although Terah is now dead, the interrupted journey must continue. So Yhwh approaches Abraham. The summons is nevertheless phrased without reference to the original plan. Instead of saying 'Get on your feet and finish off the journey your family is supposed to be making', Yhwh says 'leave your country, relations and family, to go to *somewhere I'll show you*'. Haran was not, of course, Abraham's birthplace, but perhaps he had been there long enough for it to be called 'his country'. The 'call' (it is actually a command) is backed up with an inducement: 'if you do this, I'll make you, literally, a household name, and you will be the ancestor of a great nation. Your friends will be my friends, and your enemies my enemies.' Abraham responds to this offer by going.

The narrator tells simply that they 'set out to go (יצאו ללכת) to the land of Canaan'. There are two surprises here. First is that, despite the instructions, Abraham takes his nephew, Lot, his wife, and all the people and possessions they had acquired in Haran. This is a rather generous interpretation of 'leaving kindred'! Second is that Abraham knows in which direction to go! He is not recorded as having asked 'which way should I set out?' But indeed, why should he, because he had presumably asked his father where they were headed for when they left Ur. Surely he knew that their luggage had originally been labelled 'Canaan'. Thus his heading is no surprise. We should not, then, consider Abraham either to be totally or blindly obedient. There is one other item: his wife is unable to have children (11.30).[6] The promise of many descendants is therefore mysterious. But Abraham's curiosity is not aroused. Perhaps he is faithfully leaving this to Yhwh. His subsequent actions will perhaps confirm or deny this.

So much, for the moment, for the character of Abraham. What about Yhwh? Why did he ask Abraham to leave his family, and why did he offer the inducement to leave? One possibility is that Abraham's family are being abandoned because they disobeyed their instruction to go all the way to Canaan. If so, we have another example of the ploy of abandoning a disobedient generation and moving on to the next one, as in the later wilderness journey (e.g. Num. 14.20-23). This might also explain why Yhwh is making *Abraham* the father of a nation (or nations) rather than his father Terah. Then Yhwh says to Abraham, 'go

6. The reader must realize that male infertility is unknown in the biblical world.

*to the land which I will show you'*. As we have just observed, Abraham
appears to know which land this is; does Yhwh know that he knows?
There is reticence here which it is hard to evaluate at the moment, but it
suggests a certain lack of frankness. Yhwh wants Abraham to go on a
sort of mystery tour, to trust him for directions. But Abraham refuses to
follow this, and, as we have seen, sets off in the direction he knows he
has to take. The hint of the beginning of a game between these two
characters? We shall see.

   Then there is the 'promise'. This is an important clue to Yhwh's character and behaviour, since he repeats promises throughout the story. At
this stage there is no commitment to give Abraham the land he is going
to. He will have many descendants and be blessed; others will achieve
blessing through him too. How this is to happen is not said, and the
promise is short on detail. But Yhwh for some reason thinks that
Abraham needs inducements. Whether he actually *does* need them we
shall wait to see—as we shall see how the promises vary from time to
time.

   And so even from the opening exchange, we can sniff some interesting possibilities for the development of this relationship. Far from it
being straightforward, frank and honest, it already exhibits wariness:
what Yhwh tells Abraham and what Abraham does do not suggest a
relationship of total trust either way. We cannot say yet whether this
uncertain beginning will be indicative of the relationship to come; but we
have been warned to read carefully!

   The journey itself is not described, but when Abraham passes through
Canaan and decides to stop roughly in the middle, in Shechem, the
narrator tells us abruptly that 'the Canaanites were in the land' (12.6).
This is not just a matter-of-fact observation. The phrase 'land of Canaan'
is mentioned twice in v. 5, which seems awkward. But perhaps we are
being warned of something: Canaanites! Yet who else *would* be in the
land of Canaan but Canaanites? we might ask. Perhaps the point is that
it is occupied *at all*. In Haran, Abram had been told that he would be
'shown' a land. Now he has seen it, and it is already occupied, so it will
not, presumably, be his land. Were these other settlers supposed to be
there? Was it because Terah stopped in Haran that other people on their
way from Shinar overtook him and got there first? The mention of
Canaanites complicates the reader's expectations, and Abraham's as
well, because he now realizes that he has exchanged a land where he
had lived for quite a long time for one where others have lived quite a

long time and he is a newcomer. It is not an empty land. Perhaps it is on Abraham's mind to move on. The next step (12.7) is that Yhwh declares he is going to *give* this land to Abram's descendants. The fact that Yhwh did not say this in Haran reinforces the impression that he wants to play games with Abraham, to keep him one step behind, to lure him onwards with a new promise each time. And do his new neighbours know yet that they are not going to keep this land?

Abraham's conjectured misgivings explain his reaction to this offer. He makes no speech of gratitude, like 'Oh Yhwh, you shouldn't! I don't deserve this!' Nor does he ask, 'How much land will my descendants get?' He doesn't want to know where all this leaves *him*. Possibly he is uninterested in what will come to his descendants, and more interested in what will come to him. What is *he* supposed to do while waiting for his descendants to get this unspecified amount of land at an unspecified time and by unspecified means?

Had he been content with the promise that his descendants would ultimately get this land, he might at the very least have settled there ready for his descendants to take over the place. But no: he leaves it and goes to Bethel, offers a sacrifice and moves on even further, in a southerly direction, presumably on his own initiative. Now, many animals mark their territory by dropping faeces or urine; perhaps patriarchs do it by building altars. Yet there is no clue that Abraham is claiming his descendants' land by this device, because instead of going in a circle round Canaan he heads in a fairly straight southerly direction, until he is almost at the other end of Canaan (v. 9).

The next development seems to nudge him on his already chosen route. This promised land now has no food. Famines are, from the biblical world-view, caused by gods, and so we must ask ourselves why Yhwh is now pushing his client out of the land that his descendants will own. Maybe so that he can reassure himself that he is controlling Abraham, appearing to dictate what the patriarch-to-be has decided of his own accord to do anyway? (This is a ploy Yhwh resorts to several times with Abraham, as we shall see.) So Abraham enters Egypt, but before crossing the border he asks his wife to pose as his sister, in order that he should not be killed. What does this tell us about Abraham? If he is apparently unworried about being in the land or begetting offspring, he is very worried about his own skin—worried enough to risk the life of his spouse (although at least there is no danger of her getting pregnant!) Some commentators have taken the benign view that

Abraham did not anticipate the outcome of this ruse.[7] This is possible, but rather implausible. Abraham's life is in danger, he himself says, because his wife is desirable enough for him to be killed for her possession. It follows that masquerading as a single woman will inevitably lead Sarah (I will call her Sarah, though like the two male leads she changes her name during the story) to the consequences that do in fact ensue.

For the first time in this story Abraham is openly instigating a chain of events himself, and they are entirely to his personal benefit. He does not have to say, 'You like my sister?', but in fact pimps nonetheless, and without scruple or remorse. The ruse he has instigated gives him wealth, and we shall discover that he tries the trick again later, obviously aware of its consequences for his own pocket. Because he is the legal 'owner' of his sister, he is entitled to payment in return for her services, remuneration he does not decline. 'For his sake [Pharaoh] dealt well with Abra[ha]m; and he got sheep, oxen, male donkeys, male and female slaves, female donkeys and camels' (12.16). The actions of Abram in Egypt are powerful clues to his personality, and they suggest a scheming and selfish character, not one who would follow the directions of a god without calculating the implications for himself. With hindsight, we can reconstruct a plausible motivation for his behaviour so far: he left for Canaan because that was the land his family was supposed to have; he thought it would be empty, but it has occupants already. So he goes to Egypt to make a fortune for himself instead.

Certainly he seems happy with the arrangement. Pharaoh also was presumably happy with the new addition to his harem. What Sarah feels about this is of no interest to either Abraham or the narrator. We moderns must therefore fill in for her. Perhaps she was miserable. But maybe she went along with the plan quite willingly. Maybe she was quite happy exchanging a wandering and uncaring husband for an appreciative and very rich sugar-Pharaoh. It is not impossible that the arrangement suited her too. If so, every human being in the story is happy with the arrangement.[8] So who is not happy, and how does this

---

7.   E.g. D.L. Petersen, 'A Thrice-Told Tale: Genre, Theme and Motif', *BR* 18 (1973), pp. 30-43. Naomi Sternberg, on the other hand, comments that 'Abraham knows exactly what he is doing' (*Kinship and Marriage in Genesis: A Household Economics Perspective* [Minneapolis: Fortress Press, 1993], p. 53 n. 30).

8.   Though any feminists who want a different, but fascinating explanation of Abraham's treatment of his wife can read J.C. Exum, *Fragmented Women: Feminist*

arrangement come to an end? Only Yhwh wishes it finished. Whether or not Abraham really wants his descendants, land and blessing we are not yet able to decide, but Yhwh is determined to give them to him anyway. He intervenes to stop this state of affairs developing any further. He does so not to *save* anyone or anything (as pious readers may be inclined to suppose, guided by the majority of commentators). For from *what* is anyone to be saved? Yhwh is too late to save Sarah's virtue (even if she wanted it saved), and he is saving Abraham only from the terrible fate of getting richer every day without having to work for it. The motives must lie elsewhere. It looks as if Yhwh, who has lost control of the situation, wishes to reinstate his own agenda, one which involves having Abraham in the land of Canaan and thinking about descendants. He might try to bribe Abraham to leave, or fool him into leaving. But a simpler means is employed, by which he brings about Abraham's departure plus spouse. Abraham and Sarah are banished from Egypt, so that they cannot return (and the next time they try the trick it will have to be somewhere else). Yhwh wants Abraham back in the land of Canaan. But Abraham apparently wants to be where the wealth (and the food) are, which is certainly not in Canaan. A compromise between these conflicting ambitions is called for: Abraham can get rich, but in Canaan. And this duly ensues.

Let us pause again to review the main characters and their relationship. Abraham is beginning to display himself as an unscrupulous entrepreneur, a get-rich-quick merchant, for whom long-term land possession and descendants are not important. Whatever Yhwh may want for him, *he* will pursue his own goals. Yhwh cannot, or will not, directly control Abraham, though he can bring about the fulfilment of his own plans by guile and by the divine powers he has. But the Egyptian episode shows that Abraham's interests and Yhwh's are not commensurate. The *genre* of the relationship is beginning to emerge: it is a kind of male association in which neither trusts the other, but they stick together for reasons of their own. They kid each other, they even resent each other a little, but ultimately they enjoy the games they play together. The entire relationship is like a sustained poker game in which one's own hand is concealed, and one tries to win the hand that is being played, before moving on to the next one. It is a well-known species of

*(Sub)versions of Biblical Narratives* (JSOTSup, 163; Sheffield: JSOT Press, 1993), pp. 148-69: 'Who's Afraid of "The Endangered Ancestress"'.

male bonding, in which (need it be said) women and families may well become part of the stakes.

Another conflict of interests, another round of poker, now takes place as a result of the compromise which brought Abraham back to Canaan as a rich man. Everything that Abraham has done and is going to do suggests that he is very fond of Lot, fond enough to have brought him with him to Canaan in the first place, to offer him whatever part of the land he wants, fond enough to argue with Yhwh in order to save his life, fond enough to go to war to recapture him. Abraham's general attitude makes sense if he believes Lot to be his heir.[9] But now the land promised to his countless descendants is not even big enough for him and Lot. Moreover, there is another item: the other inhabitants are also growing. The place now has not only Canaanites, but 'Canaanites and Perizzites' (13.7). Abraham therefore proposes to split it, allowing Lot the choice—perhaps assuming that Lot's descendants will have it all anyway in the end. But the story takes Lot to the wide Jordan valley while Abraham takes the rest. Moreover, Lot chooses a place where the people are wicked, 'great sinners against Yhwh' (13.13). This gives ground, or perhaps pretext, for Yhwh's dislike of Lot. Lot has included himself out. The narrator also tells us that 'Abra[ha]m dwelt in the land of Canaan', again an apparently unneccesary addition: but we are being informed that Lot does not live in Canaan any more. Whether Abraham or Lot realized this we cannot know. But the narrator wants us to realize already that Lot has made the wrong choice, and that the land will fall to other descendants of his uncle, not him. (Later on in the story, Abraham's posterity will be promised the land inhabited also by Lot's descendants, but at the moment he is not in the picture at all.)

Certainly it looks as if Yhwh has ruled Lot out. Why does Lot get kidnapped? Why does his chosen land get blitzed, with Lot himself escaping narrowly, and losing his wife? Why does Lot's line later continue only through the initiative of his daughters-in-law (19.30-38)? It is hard not to see behind all this a series of manoeuvres by Yhwh to get rid of this person and his line. All such devices, however, are foiled by other members of Lot's family, with the result that his descendants, the Ammonites and Moabites, complicate the picture for Abraham's other

---

9.    See L. Turner, *Announcements of Plot in Genesis* (JSOTSup, 96; Sheffield: JSOT Press, 1990), pp. 51-114; D.J.A. Clines, 'What Happens in Genesis', in *What Does Eve Do to Help?*, pp. 61-84 (esp. 71-73); Sternberg, *Kinship and Marriage in Genesis*, pp. 50-52.

descendants ever after. (Yhwh finally gets even with them by having Moses specifically exclude them from the congregation of Israel.) But Yhwh's move against Lot begins now. As soon as the heir apparent has gone off to his chosen territory, Yhwh says to Abraham that he will give *him*, Abraham, the land as far as he can see, and for *his* descendants— not Lot's.

Note what is happening to the promises: first no promise of land, then a promise to descendants, now a promise to Abraham himself. Is Yhwh simply revealing a little more of the plan he always had? Or is it necessary to increase the incentive to keep Abraham interested? If the latter, it is hardly a successful ploy, for again Abraham does not seem to accept it at face value. Apart from the increase in the non-Abrahamic population of Canaan, he himself has no direct descendants, and still seems to regard Lot as his only bet, which is why he will shortly rescue him. In addition to all these reservations, 'as far as he can see' is not really a very large amount of land, considering the wealth he now has. You cannot see all that far from Bethel. It is true that he is now being promised this land *personally*, but he is already making a good living in it. When we reflect upon it, as Abraham must have done, there is not much in this offer to attract him. The previous offer of land, after all, related to Shechem, which is certainly out of sight of Bethel; is that offer still valid, or has it been superseded by this one?

Note again, then, that Yhwh's offer constitutes a running theme of the Abraham story, but a fluctuating one; and that whatever form it takes, it fails to impress Abraham. His behaviour shows no sign at all of being conditioned by the prospect of huge blessings. As for the multitudes of descendants he is promised, he makes no attempt to acquire more wives and concubines. As for the land, he is invited to take a tour of this most recently promised territory, to 'walk through the length and breadth of the land' (13.17) but in a gesture of ingratitude or of lack of interest (he could have pretended) he does not accept the invitation. Instead, he moves from Bethel to Hebron, some thirty miles or so to the south. He builds another altar there and settles down for a while

It is time for Yhwh to make the next move. The first thing is to remove Lot, by having him abducted by four foreign kings. But the ploy fails, because Abraham rescues him. Now, if we read Genesis 14 carefully, we see that Lot is not the only concern of Abraham. The story speaks more about 'goods'. The enemy took all the goods of Sodom and Gomorrah and all their provision...they also took Lot...and his goods' (v. 11); Abraham brought back 'all the goods, and also brought back his kinsman Lot, with his goods (and the women and the people)' (v. 16); Abraham gave Melchizedek a tenth of everything, but even though the king of Sodom says he should keep the goods (v. 21), Abraham does not need to keep the spoils of his allies; he will just take what his own men acquired (vv. 22-24). Here is the calculation of an acquisitive, and *self-made* (with acknowledgments to Sarah, but not Yhwh!) man: in rescuing Lot he also takes the chance of enlarging his own funds; and here is the philosophy of a seriously rich man—he does not need the small change offered to him by the king. Abraham's generosity is the generosity of the extremely affluent. Affluent enough, we must remember, to look after himself with a private army. If he could defeat four foreign kings, he might even have been able to conquer the land of Canaan for himself. But what would he gain?

Having seen his ploy to remove Lot foiled, Yhwh needs to reassert some divine control over the rich and militarily powerful sheikh. So he promises, a trifle lamely, 'Do not be afraid, Abraham, I am your shield and you will have a big reward' (15.1). Yet for the first time, Abraham bothers to answer back. He asserts the obvious: he does not have a son. This comment, in the context of what we know of Abraham's character, and also coming rather late in the day, can hardly be a disguised plea. Abraham is in the driving seat at this point, and can afford a rebuke, to the effect of 'you and I know that these promises of yours are not really serious, just a game'. He even adds to the insult by telling Yhwh that *he* has already decided who his heir is going to be, one of his own slaves. Scholars have long puzzled over the mysterious 'Eliezer of Damascus' a 'slave born in my own house'. On my reading, there is little difficulty. This person has not been mentioned before, and was not Abraham's heir until this moment. Indeed, he still is not, because Lot is alive. Abraham is taunting Yhwh. He quickly runs through his enormous list of slaves, and comes up with one who was born a slave (not an enslaved freeman), and born in Damascus. Now, it happens that Abraham has just been in the vicinity of Damascus, pursuing four kings to 'Hobah, north of Damascus' (14.15) and has brought back with him all the spoils, including Lot's goods. Perhaps slaves were part of the booty captured on the expedition, and this Eliezer has *just* been acquired? That would be a stinging insult to Yhwh, making a newly acquired slave his heir! Now Yhwh had not actually mentioned descendants this time (and for the first time), which only adds to the insult: what else can he be offered? What else could Yhwh give him? What does Yhwh want to give him? If an heir is needed, he can name his own. And so the curious Eliezer comes to his lips and to our attention, only to disappear immediately without trace.

Up to this point there had been no overt confrontation, no defiance. But this provocative response, this outburst of temper is unwise, because it can destroy the delicate relationship if not immediately resolved. For gods cannot have humans saying publicly that they do not take them seriously (what humans think privately is another matter). In the thought-world of the Bible, gods need humans, but humans need gods too. So both sides need to restore equilibrium, or else the plot cannot move on and there will be no Israel and no bibles and no Western culture.

Yhwh makes the first countermove by saying that Abraham will have a son, that his seed will be as numerous as the stars. The talk about 'descendants' finally boils down to a specific promise. Abraham is mollified, or at least takes the opportunity to restore the good relations, and so he makes his gesture too: 'Abraham believed this, and it was reckoned to him as righteousness'. But precisely at this point, at the moment which in the New Testament Paul fastens on (Gal. 3.6), this belief seems to be destroyed. Only two verses later Abraham is asking for proof! What, in the intervening verse, has happened? Yhwh has told Abraham that he had called him from Ur to give him the land. For some reason, this has jolted Abraham out of his believing mode and into his proof-asking mode. Perhaps the reason is that Yhwh is misrepresenting the initial encounter with Abraham. Of course, Abraham knew that his family had really been instructed while in Ur to go to Canaan, but Yhwh had not said anything of the kind in Haran. Abraham also recalls that he was *not* originally promised the land either. He now remembers he is dealing with a duplicitous deity who cannot even put the past straight, so is unlikely to be trusted with the future. However, if we read scrupulously, we shall notice that Abraham asks for proof *that he will possess the land*, not proof of a natural heir. So Abraham is perhaps diplomatically passing over the son promise but making it clear that his trust is not to be taken for granted.

This verbal transaction marks some kind of climax in the relationship. The god has made his most concrete promise yet. Abraham may or may not believe *that*. But he has grown a little too cocky, and needs putting in his place. The sequel is therefore a sinister ballet: birds of prey come down (note that Abraham is not cowed; he scares them off); sunset sees dread and great darkness. The odd sequence has a clear purpose to it: Yhwh has to reassert the traditionally accepted right of gods to be in the driving seat, and so orchestrates a scene, in which mystery and fear will be present. He also pays back Abraham for wanting to have proof by adding to the promise a lot of small print. On the one hand he is giving the biggest description yet of the land to be acquired—from the Euphrates almost to Egypt (and that, as I commented earlier, will include Lot's territory). On the other hand, this land has now become the home not just of Canaanites, not even just of Canaanites and Perizzites, but of ten nations (15.19-21)! Furthermore, these cannot be dispossessed until the 'iniquity of the Amorites is complete' (v. 16). Therefore, notwithstanding the promises already made, the land will not come immediately to his descendants (and thus, of course, not to Abraham either!), but only four generations later. Yhwh is asserting himself; Abraham needs to know who is in control of land distribution, and that it does not pay to question promises! The deal with Abraham is part of a larger strategy involving other nations and specified but undisclosed amounts of iniquity. So Abraham's descendants *can* have the land—later, when certain other conditions have been met. The prize is now bigger but further away. Is Abraham after all justified by his lack of faith, or is Yhwh punishing him for it? But Yhwh has never issued two identical promises in a row anyway, so is Abraham unreasonable not to get too enthusiastic about them? Indeed, is he becoming weary with the recurrent promise? I get the impression that the promise is an important card in the game, though, as if Yhwh ultimately needs Abraham to accept it; that may be exactly why Abraham does not!

Are we asking ourselves whether Abraham has any right to disregard promises from gods? If so, we have to read further in the biblical story to see whether he was ultimately justified. Abraham himself will never be given any land, not so much as a square centimetre of territory, until Sarah is dead and he *buys* a cave to bury her in. If we want to check whether his descendants get their land in four generations, we need to count to the first generation of the Egyptian enslavement. The wider story endorses Abraham's doubts. But from the perspective of the characters, the future is unknown, and the issue is not really about who is 'right' but who is getting the upper hand. These are, after all, two males with every bit of male ego a male character can have.

If Abraham still believes in the promise of a natural son, he does nothing about it. Instead, it is Sarah who suggests the obvious solution, that she can have a *surrogate* child (ch. 16). The Egyptian slave, Hagar (acquired while Sarah was living with Pharaoh?) conceives, but Sarah gets second thoughts, blaming Abraham because the slave feels superior, and on Abraham's bidding sends her away. Sarah's interest in a natural heir for Abraham is in the end hardly greater than her husband's. What *is* curious is this sudden burst of assertiveness on Sarah's part, and Abraham's acquiescence. Given their previous relationship, this is unexpected. There is one way to resolve Sarah's behaviour, however: to recognize, as we suspected, that in Egypt she did not comply with her husband's request and accompany Pharaoh in a purely docile manner. Perhaps she suspected that the infertility was Abraham's and wanted to find out? As for Abraham, his ready agreement to the expulsion of Hagar only underlines his lack of ambition for a natural heir. But as it is, the heir is preserved with his mother, and returns to the household. Yhwh's messenger, who confronts Hagar, gives her the speech typically given to mothers who are to bear special children: 'you shall bear a son; you shall call his name...he shall be...' (16.11), and although his horoscope is not very promising, the external circumstances appear to lead us, or at least Sarah and Abraham, to believe that this is the heir Abraham has been promised. But it is, as we soon find out, only a game. The charade, for such it obviously is, is a piece of divine mischief, and fits in well with Yhwh's strategy of keeping Abraham on the hook. What can possibly happen next but yet another repeat, with suitable alterations, of the promise? This time a change of name is required, and the descendants will have the land for ever, and Yhwh will be their god. All males will have to be circumcised, Sarah has to change her name too, and she will be the appointed co-recipient of the divine blessing (ch. 19).

The fact that Abraham falls on his face at the beginning of this encounter ought not to signal that he is entirely submissive to Yhwh's directions. When he hears of Sarah's imminent pregnancy, he laughs, and immediately asks for *Ishmael* to be preserved and has *Ishmael* circumcised along with himself. This is not behaviour redolent of credence or obedience, but rather of disbelief, or at the very least caginess, as if to say 'let's wait and see'. He now has a natural heir, after all, and has no need of a child by Sarah. Just as previously with Lot, he prefers to stay with what he has rather than what he might (or might not) have in the future.

Faced with Abraham's attachment to Ishmael, Yhwh can only try to involve Sarah, who has recently been successful in getting her way with her husband. So the promise of a son comes to her (18.10). Like Abraham, she laughs too. Incredulity runs in the family! The time has come for another move from Yhwh.

In 18.17 the god says, no doubt in a stage whisper,

> Shall I hide from Abraham what I am about to do, seeing that Abraham shall become a great and mighty nation, and all the nations of the earth shall bless themselves by his name? No, for I have chosen him.

This is not an innocent statement: nothing that transpired between Yhwh and Abraham is ever innocent. The forthcoming announcement will have some purpose. But note the important reminder that it is Yhwh who chose Abraham and not vice versa. This is an important element in the relationship, for it gives the human a vital edge. Abraham did not choose Yhwh, nor ask for anything from him. It is Yhwh who has thrust upon Abraham the promises of land, progeny, blessing. By refusing all these, Abraham is losing nothing except the disfavour of the deity (though divine disfavour is not to be lightly entertained). But the plan for Abraham's life is Yhwh's and it is he who must bring about its fulfilment. He has not yet succeeded in making Abraham take on responsibility for it. His announcements to Abraham have been directed to the end of motivating the human to follow the plan (or prevent him from abandoning it). And so what he is now proposing to tell his chosen patriarch is designed to affect Abraham's attitude towards his posterity. So he make it clear that he is worried about what is happening in Sodom.

Nothing more needs to be said: he has Abraham's attention immediately (18.23). Abraham takes a very bold initiative indeed, and engages his deity in earnest bargaining. The conversation between them has attracted a lot of theological and ethical comment, centring on the problem of the destruction of the righteous with the wicked. But this comment ignores entirely the story of Yhwh and Abraham and the dynamics of their relationship. For what is taking place is not a debate about justice or mercy. For this one time in his whole life Abraham wants something, asks for it, and bargains, instead of his usual nonchalance. But what he wants is not the preservation of people unknown to him. No: he is interested in one particular inhabitant of the wicked city. Lot is in Sodom, and Abraham is fond of Lot; and if the city is destroyed Lot goes with it. Naturally Abraham does not say so, and is therefore concealing his real interest. But of course Yhwh knows this perfectly well too. In this negotiation, neither party is playing for the stakes they are pretending to. And each party knows the other's hand. Yhwh has decided to destroy Sodom anyway, and we learn from 19.12 that he does so. So much for the argument about saving a city for the sake of ten righteous people! But, as with the return of Abraham from Egypt, the result is a compromise. Yhwh will destroy Sodom, but save Lot. This he does reluctantly, for the text tells us (19.29) that he saved Lot for Abraham's sake, which is closer than the narrator usually gets to hinting at what his characters are really up to. But Lot loses his wife, thus making the prospect of his producing a line of male descendants for Abraham dimmer. For he has only two daughters. He also has to live in a cave, having lost his possessions and being fearful to return to Zoar. He is no catch for a new wife. Fortunately, his enterprising daughters ensure the continuation of the line. This was presumably not Yhwh's intention. But at any rate these descendants can hardly be worthy of the name of Abraham; so effectively Lot is out of the picture. Ishmael remains, of course.

And so to ch. 20, where again Abraham is in a foreign land and passing off Sarah as his sister. After the Sodom episode, Abraham feels like another hand of cards and another bluff. He provokes Yhwh with a rerun of the wife-sister game. We may wonder how serious he can be, given the fact that Sarah is past the menopause (18.11) and presumably not the most attractive of the women available to Abimelech. But we do note that Sarah is not necessarily complicit this time: she does not agree to say she is his sister, as previously, and it is Abraham who has to make the declaration. At any rate, Abimelech 'takes' her but does not have sex. However unlikely the imminent deed, Yhwh cannot afford now to let it happen, since Sarah is pregnant (or about to be) and doubts about paternity cannot be afforded. As far as Abraham is concerned, the mere hint that the child might be someone else's would give him a strong card. Yhwh must, and does, intervene to warn Abimelech and to prevent anything actually happening.

We might expect Yhwh to become angry with Abraham for this ruse. Instead, he blames the entirely innocent (if gerontophiliac) Abimelech for perpetrating a crime against Abraham! According to Yhwh, Abraham is a prophet, and he tells the ruler that Abraham will pray for him. This is a neat response: rather than acknowledge that he has lost a trick, Yhwh turns the tables by having Abimelech angrily confront Abraham with having 'done things to me that ought not to have been done' (v. 9). Put on the spot, Abraham expostulates that Sarah was really his half-sister anyway, so that there was no deception. He also puts the blame back onto the deity: 'when God caused me to wander (תעה) from my father's house...'[10] The generous Abimelech pays Abraham off, and in return Abraham prays for Yhwh to remove the infertility of all Abimelech's women. A victory for Yhwh this time: however much of a villain Abraham is, he does not want to see this kindly ruler suffer as the result of a game he is playing with his deity. So in the end he is forced to pray to Yhwh on Abimelech's behalf. Yhwh accedes: the point has been made. But this will not be the last time that an innocent male is to be victim of the games between Abraham and his god.

In the next chapter Isaac is born, and so in accordance with the plan Ishmael has to be evicted. Since it is evident that Abraham will not do this of his own accord, Yhwh has Sarah take the initiative. 'The incident was very distressing to Abraham' (21.11), but Yhwh tells him (of course) to do what Sarah wants—probably unnecessarily, since Sarah had previously been quite capable of having Abraham expel Hagar without reinforcements from above. But how could Yhwh fail to enjoy Abraham's discomfort at being left with Isaac only? So Yhwh and Sarah are delighted, and Abraham has his nose put out of joint. No doubt Sarah is also delighted that she will not be subjected to the wife-sister trick again. Abraham can console himself with the realization that at least he now has a son to pass it on to (see ch. 26!)

Yet the constant battling between these two males must continue, and having bested Abraham over Abimelech and Ishmael, Yhwh wants to go one trick further. We come to the great showpiece, Genesis 22. As often observed, the account is rather matter-of-fact, little emotion if any being described. The pathos lies, as so many critics tell us, in the reticence and the foregrounding. But this story has to be understood in a completely different way if we want to understand the motivation of the characters we have come to know. Up to this point the point-scoring between Yhwh and Abraham has reached a high pitch as each tries to manipulate the other. Abraham has generally gone along with every divine scheme, though usually without any indication that he accepted it, wanted it, cared about it. Only once or twice has he protested, and in each case

---

10. I. Rashkow (*The Phallacy of Genesis: A Feminist-Psychoanalytical Approach* [Literary Currents in Biblical Interpretation; Louisville: Westminster/John Knox, 1993], p. 47) makes the interesting suggestion that the *hiphil* of תעה might also mean 'cause to deceive', thus blaming Yhwh for his own lying.

over the wrong things (from Yhwh's point of view)—over Lot and then over Ishmael. But Abraham has also shown the ability to get his own way when it really mattered. Now Yhwh wants to 'test' Abraham, truly enough, but not in the sense of taxing his obedience, because he knows that Abraham's obedience threshold is very low. The test is of a different kind. He wants Abraham to have to show some positive feeling towards Isaac, to take emotional possession of his appointed heir, and to ask for something on Isaac's behalf; to protest, to finally admit defeat.

Yhwh sends Abraham to 'one of the hills I will tell you'—deliberately echoing the first encounter, in which Abraham had promptly followed instructions (more or less), to go to a land which he would be shown, and there sacrifice Isaac. Abraham duly begins to comply again, without a word of protest. But as with that trek to Canaan, Abraham's behaviour does not necessarily indicate blind obedience. There is a game of bluff going on, of course, because Yhwh does not want the son he has bestowed on Abraham, the Abraham he has chosen, to die. That death would shatter Yhwh's own plans. But Abraham knows this is a bluff, and he intends to call it. The weakness of the god's position is that he cares about Isaac more than Abraham does. It is Yhwh, not Abraham, who says that Isaac is the son whom Abraham loves. Abraham has never confessed such feelings. Even so, Yhwh knows that Abraham cannot go ahead. Yet equally, Abraham knows that Yhwh will not let it happen (he has only to remember that even Ishmael was rescued). The only thing to be resolved is: who will blink first? And so, when Isaac asks, 'Where is the lamb for a burnt offering?' Abraham replies, 'God will provide for himself (ירעה לו) the lamb for the offering, my son'. *There is no irony here.* Abraham is saying what he knows perfectly well to be the outcome. Perhaps he is hoping, perhaps he knows, that Yhwh is listening. His words also make a nice play on the 'seeing'—the pun on the name of the mountain (v. 14) and on the contrast of Abraham's 'seeing' (v. 4) and  hwh's seeing. It reflects in a way the issue going on between the two: who is going to 'see to' the outcome? It will not be Isaac, but something else—whatever, let Yhwh see to it. The later Jewish embellishment of this story[11] is quite right to redirect the focus of attention onto Isaac. *He* did behave very well. Rather like Abimelech, he, the one decent person, found himself suffering at the expense of a game of bluff going on between two old tricksters.

---

11. The history of the 'Aqedah' is very well surveyed in S. Spiegel, *The Last Trial* (trans. J. Goldin; New York: Random House, 1967).

Yhwh is the one who backs down. He tells Abraham to stop, not the reverse. Abraham has successfully called the bluff and won the contest. But what can Yhwh do? Deities are not supposed to lose: in the end they are not *allowed* to lose, or at least to be seen to lose. He must save face by playing his favourite card, saying in effect, 'because you have done this, you will indeed have what I promised anyway'. He must pretend that this episode was a test Abraham had to pass in order to get his promise fulfilled. He and Abraham know better, but at least the impression has been created that the deity is in charge. And that impression has largely worked: most commentators misread accordingly.

The story is nearly over. The narrator, to whom we owe the clues for the reading, gives us another one in the last four verses of the chapter, telling how many children Abraham's brother had. What good is that fecundity to Abraham, to know that while his *one* son is *not* being sacrificed after all, Nahor (who did not have to leave the family home in the first place) is busy siring *eight* sons. And the very next event, in ch. 23, is the death of Sarah. In this very male story she has played an important role, but having done the major task of a woman in a biblical story, having a male child, she can now be disposed of. She is duly buried in her own special cave. Then we have a long account of the search for a wife for Isaac. At last he will take care of his son. But there is another twist to come. For having made no move while Sarah was alive to have a natural heir, now that she is dead he remarries and sires another six sons by another wife (which, whatever else it does, confirms that Abraham was not infertile!) But he sends them all away and bequeaths everything to Isaac. Is this a final gesture of submission, acceding to the divine wish that only Isaac is to inherit? After all the games, has the old schemer given in? He is, after all, very old and very blessed and perhaps very tired. All he has left to do is die.

The ending is a proper one. There are no fights left to be had: the issue of succession is settled; the point of the game is over. It is right and proper that every human should finally make peace with their deity. Humans are mortal beings, unlike gods, and however cleverly a human may deal with a god, the truth is that death comes to us and not to them.

We readers might reflect that he dies with the promised heir, but with no land except what he is buried in, which he had to buy, and with no especial blessing for him or anyone. The promises from his god did not come to much in his own lifetime, and the ongoing story will tell us how far they worked out for his successors.

Who left us this story? What was its author, or what were its authors, trying to say? Were they entertaining us with an epic of a tussle between their god and an ancestor of theirs who was his match? Certainly, the story is clever, entertaining, humorous, sometimes ambiguous, and with a suitably downbeat ending. The ploys that Abraham and Yhwh use against each other are amusing and perhaps believable. But we must remember that we are dealing with characters only, not with real persons or events. Even if there were an Abraham or a Yhwh, we cannot assume that they correspond to what this story has them be or do. There are no historical or theological truths that need to be won from this, only the wisdom and experience of the tellers. It is not at all clear that the story intended to convey theological dogmas. If so, it is hard to identify what they are. Abraham is certainly no model father or husband, and Yhwh no model god.

But one can suggest the sort of reactions that this story might have conveyed to the readers for whom it was intended—whoever they were. The story says to them: do not trust a deity. He or she or it almost certainly does not trust you, and has no reason to tell you the truth. Gods are in the business of making promises and these are rarely fulfilled. Abraham did not achieve his imposed ambition of populating the area between the Nile and the Euphrates, and his descendants have not received conspicuous blessings over the years. Deities, like politicians, like to keep humans dangling in the hope of things to come, promises renewed, altered, repeated. But be wise like Abraham. Take all that your deity says with a pinch, if not a pillar, of salt. Their strong card is our belief and trust in them. If we really believe in what they say, we may lose. But if we call their bluff, and while pretending to go along with them, keep our own counsel, set our own goals, we can remain in charge of our own lives. Whatever they decide to give us, let them give it. If they want to bless us, let us not object, but let it not deter us from our own course or seduce us into grovelling gratitude. This philosophy will probably not suit a modern Christian or Jew, and it is irrelevant to an atheist. But let us hear it, anyway, and wonder at what kind of experiences or imaginations nourished such a wonderful narrative.[12]

12. A different and shorter reading of the story of Abraham and Sarah, which nevertheless makes some of the same observations as here (and can be recommended for comparison) is in D.M. Gunn and D.N. Fewell, *Narrative in the Hebrew Bible* (Oxford: Oxford University Press, 1993), pp. 90-100.

Chapter 6

## 'TAKE IT TO THE LORD IN PRAYER':
## THE PEASANT'S LAMENT

> Religious distress is at the same time the expression of real distress and
> the protest against real distress. Religion is the sigh of the oppressed
> creature, the heart of a heartless world, just as it is the spirit of a spiritless
> situation... It is the fantastic realization of the human essence because the
> human essence has no reality. (Karl Marx)[1]

> Since every need for salvation is an expression of some distress, social or
> economic oppression is an effective source of salvation beliefs, though by
> no means the exclusive source. Other things being equal, classes with high
> social and economic privilege will scarcely be prone to evolve the idea of
> salvation. Rather they assign to religion the primary function of legit-
> imizing their own life pattern and situation in the world. (Max Weber)[2]

It is well-known among practitioners and readers of sociology that
religions perform social functions, and cannot be isolated as self-
contained systems of belief or practice operating independently of the
social and economic forces that control the world we live in as members
of human societies. Such a view would in any case be quite contrary to
the ideology of the biblical literature, or the great bulk of it, in which
visions of an ideal world are expressed in terms of economic and social
harmony, where divine laws address social and economic welfare, where
political rulers are represented as divine agents, and rewards and punishments for religious failings express themselves in political, economic and
social measures.

Nevertheless, personal piety and individual salvation are important

---

1. 'Contribution to the Critique of Hegel's Philosophy of Right' (1844), cited
from *Marx and Engels on Religion* (New York: Schocken Books, 1964), pp. 41-42
(and also cited in R.A. Horsley, *Jesus and the Spiral of Violence: Popular Jewish
Resistance in Roman Palestine* [Minneapolis: Fortress Press, 1993], p. 33).
2. M. Weber, *The Sociology of Religion* (ET; New York: Beacon Press, 1963).

elements in the belief and practice of most Christians, and communication between them and their god (but not so obviously the reverse) often takes place in personal prayer or within church worship, as well as, less commonly, in immediate confrontation with wider political or social settings. Not surprisingly, then, the Psalms are often for Christians the most popular book of their Old Testament. They appear as the most intimate and revealing corpus of Israelite/Judaean religious sentiment, where the distress, joy, confidence, fear and celebration of individual and corporate worshippers is expressed in what is often fine poetry. Modern Jewish and Christian readers sometimes find themselves able to express their own religious feelings through the words of the Psalms more eloquently than in their own. Divorced from whatever concrete situations may have engendered them, and from whatever specific distresses or jubilations they may have once addressed, the Psalms are capable of a universal application, or even of specific reapplication, and can provide words for a number of occasions (as indeed they did on a famous episode in the Gospels, where the opening words of Ps. 22 are placed on the lips of the crucified Jesus).[3]

Psalm 22 is what is classified as an 'individual lament', a genre which comprises about one third of the entire Psalter, and which I shall be focusing on in this chapter.[4] Attending to the specifics of the 'individual lament',[5] the reader will be aware of recurrent sets of circumstances attendant upon the ancient lamenter, and expressed by the ancient psalmist.[6] Thus, the lamenter of Psalm 6 asks for healing from an illness;

3.     Mk 15.34 and parr.

4.     Although some minor disagreement exists, the following psalms are usually assigned to this group: 9+10; 13; 17; 22; 25–28; 31; 35; 37; 38–39; 42+43; 51–52; 54–57; 59; 61; 64; 69–71; 77; 86; 88; 102; 109; 120; 130; 139–43.

5.     For recent treatment of these poems, see C. Westermann, *Praise and Lament in the Psalms* (Edinburgh: T. & T. Clark, 1981); E. Gerstenberger, *Der bittende Mensch* (Neukirchen: Neukirchener Verlag, 1980); C.C. Broyles, *The Conflict of Faith and Experience in the Psalms: A Form-Critical Theological Study* (JSOTSup, 52; Sheffield: JSOT Press, 1989). Gerstenberger's study makes an important contribution to the issue under discussion here, since he is interested in the social context of the lament, the social class of the lamenter and the ritual by which it is brought. However, his suggestion that the majority of the Psalms come from a local religious gathering (e.g. synagogue) posits an entirely unknown context. It is nevertheless not improbable that rituals of petition took place in local communities.

6.     I retain the conventional term 'lament' despite its rather technical and perhaps archaic character. There is dispute about the best terminology. By 'lamenter' I mean the implied speaker; by 'psalmist' I mean the (poetic) author.

Psalms 7, 10 and 13 ask for deliverance from enemies; Psalm 22's speaker laments verbal and physical persecution; and Psalm 27 complains of false testimony. Some lament psalms close with thanks for divine help in such predicaments. In many cases, however, the language is rather vague and general. The most common self-designation in the Psalms is עני, which can be translated as 'poor' 'afflicted', 'oppressed', and is used 41 times.[7] The word אביון, which more properly designates economic hardship (though it later acquired an ethical rather than economic connotation), occurs 23 times. Most occurrences of these terms are in psalms of individual lament.[8]

The lament usually includes a request for remedy, and is not merely an outpouring of feelings. Sometimes the deity is accused of being negligent (e.g. Pss. 6; 35; 39). Religious people in modern times sometimes regard prayer less as a vehicle for specific requests and more as an experience of communication with their god, in which they can share their troubles without necessarily expecting direct action in response. But this would hardly be an adequate account of ancient prayer. Humans before the 'age of science' believed that rains, and therefore famine, were controlled from the gods, as were pestilence and (to some degree) warfare, and accordingly so were the vicissitudes of the individual's life. There are a number of features of the human condition which nowadays we assign to natural or mechanical operations, and seek to control as humans. But in cases where the cause is divine will and not natural law, prayer is a rational intervention intended to procure remedy from the source with the authority and power to act, whether the distress be a personal one, such as illness or injustice, or a communal one, such as drought or invasion.

We are dealing, then, with a society in which certain spheres were ascribed to divine influence where nowadays we would seek natural or human causation. We might, out of habit, or as children, pray for good weather, but do not really believe that the outcome will be manipulated by the god we beseech in order to fulfil our own personal wishes. The religious among us may, with more conviction, pray for healing, but we

---

7. In Pss. 9, 10, 12, (14), (18), 22, 25, 31, (34), 35, (37), 40, 44, (68), 70, (72), 74, (82), 86, 88, 102, (107), 109, (119), 140 (those not classified as a 'lament psalm', whether individual or communal, are in parentheses; Ps. 40.13-17 is often identified as a lament).

8. In Pss. 9, 12, 35, (37), 40, (49), 69, 70, (72), 74, (82), 86, (107), 109, (112), (113), (132), 140 (those in parentheses are not individual or communal laments).

also acknowledge that illness has non-divine causes and that medical or surgical treatment plays a major and perhaps more important role. Both religious and nationalistic people may pray for victory in war, but rationally many of these will know that they are asking for the moral and physical courage necessary for victory. In such prayers religious people may be able to use psalms, but their expectations will be different from those of the original users of these poems. Their requests are no longer as 'rational' as they once were.

Now, the division of responsibilities in ancient 'pre-scientific' societies between deities and other, human agencies is not necessarily so innocent as the preceding comments imply, nor are such societies so bereft of scientific instinct in dealing with questions raised by the laments of the Psalms, as I will argue later. There is a political dimension to such divisions. Even in our modern world, Habermas has commented that states divide reality into sacred and profane; the rationality that benefits systemic efficiency occupies the profane only; problems in the profane world such as injustice and inequality are 'referred' to the sacred.[9] The idea, whether or not we wish to apply it rigidly, is a useful one and can be applied to the world from which the Psalms originate. We have in the Psalms the language of the 'sacred' which speaks of injustice and inequality, and of distress that can be alleviated or removed by divine action. But this is a world of ideology, and once we begin to recreate a *Sitz im Leben* for these writings, we find ourselves negotiating with the 'profane' world, in which they are written and performed, and in particular with a rational economic system in which these mechanisms of lament play a role.

Let us look briefly at this system. The society in which these laments were composed was one in which the majority of people were tied to the land, either as free farmers, tenants, debt-workers, or slaves. The state (whether a local monarchy or distant imperial power or both) to which they were subject took from them taxes in the form of revenue, and in addition the sanctuary (let us say the Temple in Jerusalem) required further taxes in the form of tithes, first-born offerings, and other occasional sacrifices. The court itself (royal or priestly), and the extensive retainer classes of both court and Temple (administrators,

9. J. Habermas, 'Toward a Reconstruction of Historical Materialism', and 'Legitimation Problems in the Modern State', in *Communication and the Evolution of Society* (trans. T. McCarthy; Oxford: Polity Press, 1984 [German 1976]), pp. 130-77, 178-205.

scribes, messengers, soldiers, priests) were supported by revenues from this income, as well as by the direct income from lands owned by the monarch and the Temple. (In the case of a foreign overlord, Assyrian, Babylonian or Persian, tribute or taxes would also need to be paid over by the local regime.) As far as we can tell, the system extracted virtually all surplus wealth from the farmers in order to support the state apparatus which was located in the cities. The level of transfer of wealth from farmer to state apparatus was not ideally calculated by blind greed or hostility, but was essentially rational: the stability of this system depended on the peasants remaining alive and productive but not in possession of surplus wealth, while for their part they were perhaps willing to forfeit (some?) surplus in return for some law enforcement, political stability and protection against banditry and invasion (though banditry was presumably their own means of escape from exorbitant oppression!)

The extent of literacy in such a society is hard to establish and is disputed.[10] But it seems safe to suggest that the Psalms themselves are the product of a rather small class who were not only literate in the sense of being able to write or read their name but also in being able to compose poetry according to the conventional forms, in the accepted terminology that a deity would understand. The authors of such compositions were most probably professional scribes. It follows that the actual author of a lament psalm is likely in most if not all cases to be other than the person on whose behalf the petition is being presented. Moreover, it

---

10. On the levels of literacy in ancient Israel, see A. Millard, 'An Assessment of the Evidence for Writing in Ancient Israel', in *Biblical Archaeology Today* (Jerusalem: Israel Exploration Society and Israel Academy of Sciences in association with the American Schools of Oriental Research, 1985), pp. 301-12. A. Demsky and M. Bar-Ilan, 'Writing in Ancient Israel and Early Judaism', in M.J. Mulder (ed.), *Miqra* (CRINT; Assen: Van Gorcum; Philadelphia: Fortress Press, 1988), pp. 1-38; Millard and Demsky posit a relatively high rate of literacy, but much of the evidence is based on accepting inner-biblical data, and their definition of 'literacy' includes the ability to read and write one's name, which is far from the ability to write a poem. For an attempt to gauge the level of literacy in ancient Egypt, see J. Baines, 'Literacy and Ancient Egyptian Society', in *Man* (London: Royal Anthropological Institute of Great Britain and Ireland, 1983), pp. 572-99. He gives a figure of 1% 'in most periods'. Even allowing for the possibility that an alphabet is easier to learn than a hieroglyphic system, ease of writing is only one factor in the spread of literacy, and not necessarily an important one. Literacy is a cultural and not merely a technical phenomenon. It is, I think, generally accepted by biblical scholars that the peasant culture of Palestine in the Iron Age and Persian period was oral.

will very probably have been presented to the deity not by the lamenter but by a servant of the god, that is a priest, and at a local or national sanctuary. There is, furthermore, a widely-held view among scholars that some kind of statement of reassurance that the complaint had been heard (a kind of receipt) was also delivered to the lamenter, as a result of which sometimes an expression of thanks or confidence in a right outcome would be appended.[11]

It is important, nevertheless, to pay attention to the formalities of the psalm compositions, and to their widely-recognized stereotypical features. These features no more detract from the potential eloquence of the psalm than the demands of the sonata form on the symphonies of Haydn or Mozart. But they do highlight the conventional nature of the petition process, and guard us against imagining that through the language itself we are in direct contact with specific instances of personal distress, beautiful though the language may sometimes be. Neither specificity nor eloquence of language are proof of reality of experience; we are, after all, dealing with the art of poets! In fact, the specifics are rather rare, while the language is sometimes rather less impressive in classical Hebrew than in the translation of the KJV. The language of the Psalms is evidence of the discourse of formal lament in Judah, as is the case with other civilizations which produced them, notably the cultures of Mesopotamia. But it is unlikely that the Psalms arise directly out of the experience which they serve—indeed, if they were used more than once, they could hardly be anything of the sort. Not only are psalmist and lamenter different people, but, as it seems, the experiences of the individual lamenter are not necessarily reproduced in a specially-composed poem, but may be expected to converge with one or other stereotypical poem ready to hand.[12]

We must, of course, beware of insisting that these probabilities and inferences are fact. These Psalms, moreover, have not necessarily been collected in the form in which they were originally composed. The formation of the Psalter in its later shapes suggests its development into

11. The view was most strongly advocated by J. Begrich 'Das priesterliche Heilsorakel', *ZAW* 52 (1934), pp. 81-92, and remains widely supported.

12. The strong possibility exists that several psalms are scribal literary exercises in a traditional genre, perhaps composed in a scribal school, or even for 'serious entertainment' as poetry. This can only be suspected; we can, on the other hand, assume that the genre itself arose, and probably continued to function, in a specific context of individual petition.

a collection for private study rather than a 'hymn-book' for the Second Temple (as conceivably earlier collections of psalms may have been).[13] Yet if any of these individual laments were ever used as a vehicle of expression of particular, genuine situations of distress it is worth asking about the original production and recitation of laments in ancient Judah. And since the laments often implicate economic factors, it is realistic to implicate the economics of the process of lament itself.

For scribes need paying: their literary skill and their time do not come free. The service has to be profitable. The lamenter surely had to make a payment, probably in the form of an offering and probably in kind.[14] And payment is the point in the transaction in which the 'sacred' and the 'profane' (from our point of view, not the ancient participants') intersect. For on the 'sacred' level the offering is an inducement to the deity to respond to the petition. On the 'profane' level it is a fee to the establishment through whose means such petition can be made, and can be made efficacious. From the emic point of view payment to a priest is payment to the god; from the etic it is the transfer of wealth from one individual to another or to a corporation, or even to the state.

The emic and etic analyses of the transaction extend, or can be made to extend, to the wider issue of causation and responsibility to which I referred earlier. Emically, the petitioner is interpreted as addressing the plea (or having a functionary address it) to the deity who has the power to answer it, thus acknowledging its power over sickness, persecution, slander, sorcery, and so on. From the etic point of view, the petitioner patronizes the religious establishment as the only reliable means of communication with a deity whose power over the symptoms of the complaint would not be endorsed by the observer. Instead, the observer might recognize a means whereby divine powers are used to procure income for the privileged class. And from whom is such income

13. See, e.g., G.H. Wilson, *The Editing of the Hebrew Psalter* (Chico, CA: Scholars Press, 1983).

14. The Psalms make little mention of sacrificial acts (so Rogerson in J.W. Rogerson and P.R. Davies, *The Old Testament World* [Cambridge: Cambridge University Press; Englewood Cliffs, NJ: Prentice-Hall, 1989]; cf. K. Seybold, *Introducing the Psalms* [ET; Edinburgh: T. & T. Clark, 1990], pp. 82-85). There are a few references to sacrifices (not necessarily accompanying the petition) in, e.g., Pss. 4.5, 20.3 and 54.6, though the literary evidence of payment accompanying petitions is slim. My argument is based largely on inference, and I would not necessarily expect to find reference to payment or offering in the text of a petition itself, especially if later adapted for non-cultic use, as the Psalter was in its present form.

derived? Who are the lamenters? At times, perhaps, the privileged and wealthy of the society, but surely also the less well-off, whose need for divine assistance would be greater without the means to secure the necessary influence to assist in a favourable judgment. Perhaps the frequent self-designation as 'poor' and 'oppressed' is merely conventional language of persuasion, intended to demean one's status in the eyes of a deity whose sympathy was not to be taken for granted. But is it likely that this system of formal complaint was confined to the privileged classes? I think we can assume that the real 'underprivileged' and the real 'poor' had occasion to seek redress from their deity too, and used these psalms, or psalms like them, to address their heavenly patron.

From this point in the analysis onwards, the critic will likely cease to become a dispassionate observer of the reconstructed process of lament and begin to apply values of her or his own to it. A Christian may well accept that there is a god who has a concern for those who lament and has, in some way, power to respond, so that despite the economic aspects of the lament system, it is not a vain enterprise. Nevertheless, some Christians, together with socialists, Marxists (and perhaps others too) will find it distasteful that a system in which ostensibly the wrongs done to the 'oppressed' are being righted is simultaneously a mechanism by which the goods of poorer and less powerful people are being donated to those who are better off and not oppressed at all.

At any rate, without prejudice to religious beliefs in this or that god, we can suggest that this particular mechanism for remedying evils, in which deities are held up as accountable for certain situations of oppression and besought with the aid of the priestly establishment, is part of the very system that helps to create and sustain the conditions of oppression. Under the cloak of a theocratic economy in which justice, wealth, life, death, health, fertility and social esteem are the ultimate responsibility of deities who can be accessed only by means of a privileged institution stands an economic system created by humans themselves, in which a small elite sustains itself at the expense of the productive majority whose surpluses are removed, leaving them economically powerless and physically weaker than they would otherwise be—not to mention ideologically dominated, so as to fail to see that their oppression is the outcome of a certain social system, and indeed to cooperate with that system in attributing blame for many ills on the deity, collaborating with their exploiters in bringing to this deity problems for which humans, and not deities, are responsible.

Thus, although used positively for Jewish and Christian devotion, when considered from the point of view of their social production, the lament psalms can appear as texts that once sustained a system of economic and ideological oppression. By denying the real causes of that oppression, namely the very system by which scribes and priests were able to learn to write and make money from sacrifices and revenue from Temple property, and by deflecting responsibility onto the deity, such privileged groups were concealing the true nature of the systemic oppression from which the lamenters were suffering. By themselves benefitting from the very procedure of lament, these self-proclaimed mediators of the request for cure were actually adding further oppression.

It would not, then, be unfair to conclude that if the foregoing analysis is correct, psalms of lament were once texts of oppression in which the privileged psalmist speaks on behalf of the lamenter of whom he is himself an oppressor! Now, while it is easy to be offended at such a system in itself (which, after all, has been reconstructed by a twentieth-century scholar) one's evaluation of the beneficiaries of this process, including the psalmists themselves, will depend on whether we can rightly accuse them of wilful or conscious exploitation or should rather conclude that they, as much as the lamenters, honestly believed in the efficacy of the system from which they derived their superior standard of living. There can be no simple answer to this, as a brief survey of evidence from the biblical literature will show. What will emerge from a rough survey of the literature is an uneasy ambiguity about the reasons for poverty and the attitudes and practices to be adopted towards it.

We can begin an analysis of the ideology of poverty in the Jewish bible by exploring the book of Proverbs. This is because Proverbs is both complex in its attitude and has a slightly more explicit account of poverty than other biblical texts.[15] First of all, it does not espouse a straightforward view of poverty. Poverty is to be pitied ('the poor are avoided even by their neighbours, but the rich have many friends' [14.20]), but where it befalls one as a consequence of folly, it can be condemned ('lazy hands make one poor, but industrious hands bring wealth' [10.4]). The rich are advised not to scoff at the poor ('whoever

15.  The origin of Proverbs in popular folk-wisdom remains a possibility, but the textual evidence links them with kings and a well-off young man seems to be the implied reader. At any rate, the *literary* outcome is a product of the literate and so we can link its ideology to this social stratum.

mocks the poor shows contempt for their maker; whoever gloats over misfortune will not go unpunished' [17.5]), but to treat the poor justly ('whoever oppresses the poor shows contempt for their maker, but whoever is kind to the needy honours him' [14.31]). Poverty, then, is a pitiful state, one into which a fool may fall, but not, apparently, one that necessarily bespeaks indolence or foolishness. The poor fool may be despised, but the poor are as much creatures of the god as the rich, and generally deserve generous treatment.

There is no automatic equation here of virtue with riches or of poverty with foolishness or wickedness. Indeed, the opposite, even if as an exception proving an unstated rule, is asserted often enough: 'a poor person's field may produce abundant food, but injustice sweeps it away' (13.23); 'a poor person pleads for mercy, but a rich one answers harshly' (18.23); 'better a poor person whose walk is blameless than a fool [implied as rich?] whose lips are perverse' (19.1). The poor may be industrious; they may be made poorer by injustice, and may be exploited by the rich. It is therefore impossible to impose on Proverbs a rigid retributional ideology of poverty. Its moral universe of just reward and punishment controls its discourse, because as a general rule wisdom brings success (and that means material goods and social esteem),[16] but this does not mean that according to its principles every rich person is wise or good and every poor person foolish or wicked. The poor can, it seems, as well as becoming poor through their own indolence, also experience impoverishment through the injustice of the more powerful. Despite the overarching view that wisdom tends to riches and foolishness to poverty, Proverbs collectively resists the notion that there is a mechanical law which inexorably drives virtue towards wealth; nor does the possession of wealth attest virtue.

Yet, while some can be made poor or poorer by their fellows, in the end, there is no concern in Proverbs to remove poverty. The existence of poverty is not an ethical problem. The rich can help, and should take pity, take care not to oppress, and even give sustenance. But their own wealth and others' poverty are not in any way connected. There is no apparent awareness that their own wealth has anything at all to do with the poverty of others. The poor are not their responsibility other than as occasions for charity and justice. The justice entailed in the existence of poverty and wealth side by side in society is a matter for the deity, not

16. How this mechanism works is not important here: cf. K. Koch, 'Gibt es ein Vergeltungsdogma im AT?', *ZTK* 52 (1955), pp. 1-42.

for human society itself. Poverty is not perceived, generally, as a product of any economic system, but as a law of nature. Personal poverty may be caused by human action, but the condition of poverty generally is not. To redeem the poor from poverty is not among the obligations laid on humans, according to Proverbs. The ideal society is not one in which poverty does not exist, or at least there is nothing in Proverbs to suggest that this idea occurred to anyone.

A similar ambiguity towards poverty exists in legal texts. On the one hand, measures to alleviate poverty such as leaving some harvest ungathered (Lev. 19.10; 23.22; and Exod. 23.11 on leaving all seventh-year produce to the poor) are enjoined. The poor are permitted to make less valuable offerings (Lev. 14.21; 27.8) and there are regulations for the redemption of property (Lev. 25.25). On the other hand, poverty is something that will always exist (Deut. 15.11), and it is, as with Proverbs, the business of the deity to remove (or inflict) it; his blessings can ensure its disappearance (Deut. 15.4). Hence the refuge of the poor is ultimately with their god and not elsewhere, as we repeatedly find in the Psalms too (14.6; 34.6; 40.17; 68.10; 70.5[17]).

We would, to be fair, hardly expect otherwise in a culture where there is no science of economics (if 'science' is the right word), where the creation and distribution of wealth are not amenable to theoretical and empirical analysis and where, it seems, one person's wealth is not a function of another's lack of it. Poverty, a situation which a majority of the population of an ancient agrarian society experienced, with hunger, disease and premature death as a recurrent possibility through famine, war or over-exploitation, was part of the created order; and while there is some evidence of concern to avoid an exacerbation of poverty, or its exploitation, poverty itself is not a symptom of an unjust system.

And yet, most twentieth-century readers of bibles believe that the distribution of wealth from wealth-producing people to wealth-absorbing people is not a matter of indifference but something that humans are responsible for, and that they are obliged to resist. Drought is a natural disorder, but resultant famine is not (the story of Joseph recognizes that prudent administration can prevent it), and numerous texts throughout the biblical literature recognize that to a certain degree individual human acts not only intensify poverty but can create it. One well-known example is the creation of large estates or latifundia: 'woe to you who

---

17. Versification according to English, not Hebrew, bibles.

add house to house and join field to field till no space is left and you live alone in the land' (Isa. 5.8). Yet what is the remedy?

> Yhwh of hosts has declared in my hearing: 'Surely the great houses will become desolate, the fine mansions left without occupants. A ten-*semed* vineyard will produce only a *bath* of wine, a *homer* of seed only an *ephah* of grain.' (5.9-10).

How will this remove poverty? Amos, a book that criticizes the rich for their injustice, can offer only invasion, death, the devastation of the country and the exile of the ruling classes as consolation to those suffering oppression from the rich. The book is, of course, addressing the rich (of whatever period of time the contents were written) and perhaps attempting to threaten them into alleviating their abuse of the poor. But, we may want to ask, what benefit do the poor get from this? Rarely do we find expressed hopes of a reversal of estate in which poor become rich and rich poor—but it is there to be found (1 Sam. 2.1-10, inspiring Lk. 1.46-55). These as yet unfulfilled hopes are not widely expressed in the biblical literature, perhaps because it is the privileged from whom the literature comes, and exalting the poor at the expense of the rich is not an appetizing solution.

In the end, it is better in the eyes of the ancient writers to leave the problem of poverty in the realm of the 'sacred'. As Job says, 'Yhwh gave and Yhwh took away' (Job 1.21); indeed the whole story of Job deals with divine responsibility for human wealth (and health), which it takes for granted. In this, it merely reinforces the ambivalence of almost the entire biblical literature. Humans can make other humans poor, and can also make them a little more or a little less poor, but ultimately the fact of poverty itself rests with Yhwh. Where human responsibility is exhausted (or even where it is not), recourse to the deity is appropriate.

Is it an underlying ignorance, and thus neglect, of the ability of social and economic structures to create and to remove poverty, that differentiates the economic world-view of the biblical literature from ours? Is it that, as Godelier puts it,

> the monopoly of means (to us imaginary) of reproduction of the universe and life must have preceded the monopoly of the visible means of production, i.e. of those means which everyone could and had to produce in order to reproduce, given their relative simplicity.[18]

18. J. Godelier, 'Infrastructure, Societes and History', *Current Anthropology* 19 (1978), pp. 763-68, 767.

Partly, perhaps. But how far is it due to the sheer unwillingness of the privileged elite to acknowledge that to remove poverty would mean to abandon their own privilege? For given the feudal economic system of ancient Judah, the wealth created by the poor could never be left for them to enjoy. But their poverty, the inevitable consequence of others' wealth, was also the wellspring of much of their lamenting. They were imprisoned not only by an economic system but also by a religious belief in which prayer to the deity could amend individual grievances, but no hope of the ending of poverty as a necessary by-product of a social system was envisaged: their poor estate, as that of the rich, was ordered by the deity who presided over both rich and poor, and over the system too.

Etic readings, then, do not necessarily deprive us of ethical dimensions of reading, and emic ones are no way out of such challenges. A careful reading of the whole of the biblical literature can show an ambiguity in the attitude to economic inequality which may suggest that the uneasiness of modern readers with the mechanisms of complaint in the Psalms finds echoes in that literature. Even if devotional and critical approaches to the Psalms can be, and should be, separated, there remains plenty of scope for even the modern Jewish or Christian critic to find a way of accommodating the two without recourse to ethical schizophrenia. In Sheffield, many of the large houses built by Victorian industrialists on the salubrious western slopes of the city, leeward of the wind and distant from the polluting factories and the grimy rows of workers' houses are now divided into student flats. There is a delight to be gained from a realization that in a more democratic and egalitarian time symbols of the past can be deconstructed and rebuilt to affirm new values. Equally, the biblical Psalms can be read by poor and rich, exploited and unexploited, and by believer and non-believer. Having an origin within an evil system does not preclude the capacity for subsequent benefit. But the social origin of the psalms of lament ought not to be forgotten in the midst of the subsequent recontextualizing. For this too can teach a moral lesson to believer and non-believer: gods (real or imaginary) should not be made scapegoats for social structures that arise from human greed and thoughtlessness.

Chapter 7

DANIEL SEES THE DEATH OF GOD

Daniel is universally held to be an optimistic message in a time of great distress, insisting on the ultimate victory of the divine purpose and exhorting its readers to remain true to their religion. The more I have become engaged with this writing the less convinced have I become that this reading is anything but superficial. The message just described is indeed conveyed, but in an ambiguous manner. I shall try in the following pages to explain that the book of Daniel (I mean the version found in the Jewish bible)[1] can be interpreted as a reflection on the death of 'God'—I mean, of course, a *particular* god—and, with 'those who are wise and shall understand', it offers a diagnosis that contradicts its superficial sanguinity. The consequences of the death of their god for the people of Judah and for history are clearly foreseen, though, like Daniel's riddles and visions, this message is secluded.

The structure of the book of Daniel, as is widely recognized, falls into two parts with ch. 7 as the midpoint.[2] The formal indicators are quite obvious: this chapter is linked to chs. 2–6 by being in Aramaic, unlike chs. 8–12, but is also linked to chs. 8–12 by being a first-person account of a vision of Daniel, unlike chs. 2–6.[3] However, an equally important

1. The versification in Protestant bibles sometimes differs from the Hebrew/Aramaic. I shall use the versification of the Protestant bible unless indicated otherwise.

2. There remains uncertainty about the compositional history of the Hebrew/Aramaic book of Daniel, and this chapter is widely supposed to represent a distinct stage in its evolution. For the most recent survey of the composition of Daniel, see J.J. Collins, *Daniel* (Hermeneia; Minneapolis: Fortress Press, 1993), pp. 24-38.

3. The structure of the book of Daniel in its MT form shows some signs of having evolved into its present form rather than being composed initially. See, e.g., the intriguing suggestion of J. Lust ('The Septuagint Version of Daniel 4–5', in *The Book of Daniel in the Light of New Findings* [BETL, 106; Leuven: Peeters, 1993], pp. 39-53) that an Aramaic *Vorlage* of the LXX (not Theodotion) contained stories in

feature of the story of ch. 7 is its marking of an irrevocable transition in the divine administration of the world and its history. Chapter 7, we might say, deals with what is now fashionably called 'succession management', though from the point of view of the humans who have to live that history 'mismanagement' might be a better description. In this vision the old god, whom the book usually calls Elyon ('Most High'), hands over sovereignty to one who is not named, but described, indeed characterized, as having a human form (כבר אנש). To this character in human form is given 'dominion and glory and kingdom, that all peoples, nations, and languages should serve him; his dominion is an everlasting dominion, which shall not pass away, and his kingdom one that shall not be destroyed' (7.14). The language alludes to the dominion that earthly kings have enjoyed (see 3.4) and which is also given and taken away by Elyon (4.32), and the scenario appears to fulfil the promise of 2.44 that an indestructible kingdom will finally crush all other kingdoms.[4]

This transfer of sovereignty to the humanlike recipient, then, is no temporary measure, but for eternity. Here Elyon is not sub-contracting his world dominion to another human emperor, but permanently relinquishing it. The old god, whose title עתיק ימין connotes both his age (which, as I shall argue, is a key allusion) and his primordiality, had presumably ruled the cosmos from its beginning, and presumably the new ruler will take over until its end. It would not be over dramatic, therefore, to conclude that Daniel 7 narrates a rupture in the fabric of eternity, the single turning-point of the whole of time. It is indeed a mythic episode of the highest import, and implies a thesis about history far more radical than anything encountered in any other biblical book.

The conventional interpretation of this vision does not quite follow the foregoing assessment. Rather, commentators have taken it for granted that the vision relates to the end of history, when the four great world

the (chiastic) sequence chs. 2–3–4–7–5–6 + Bel and the Dragon. According to Lust this version is pre-Maccabean. I am dubious that ch. 5 is pre-Maccabean; the similarities between Belshazzar and Antiochus IV, and the shared theme of desecration, plus the unusually sombre ending with the king's death suggest to me that, unlike chs. 2–4 and 6, it reflects a post-165 BCE perspective. See my *Daniel* (OTG; Sheffield: JSOT Press, 1985), pp. 48-50. But opinions vary widely on the relative dating and composition of this chapter; see J. Goldingay, *Daniel* (WBC; Dallas: Word Books, 1989), pp. 104-106.

4.    H. Kvanvig, *Roots of Apocalyptic: The Mesopotamian Background of the Enoch Figure and of the Son of Man* (WMANT; Neukirchen–Vluyn: Neukirchener Verlag, 1988), p. 487 suggests that this figure may parallel Nebuchadnezzar.

empires are brought together and judged. It is an 'eschatological' scene in which the eternal deity Elyon delegates the sovereignty that, in their view, remains always his own, to a subordinate figure. The identity of this figure, the 'humanoid', has, however, long been controversial. Early Christian interpretations saw Jesus Christ, an identification still embraced by many Christian readers. For many scholars he is a symbol of the people of Israel, just as the beasts he supersedes are symbols of empires. Such a reading appears to gain support from ch. 2, which has clearly inspired ch. 7, and which foresees the 'god of heaven' setting up a kingdom, in the wake of four previous kingdoms, 'which shall never be destroyed, nor shall this kingdom be passed to another people' (2.44). The implication, for most scholars, is that this kingdom refers to the hegemony of the people of Israel. Accordingly, the 'humanoid' of ch. 7 represents the people of Israel, its human form contrasting significantly with the animal forms with which the preceding kingdoms are symbolized.

On this reading (which I have previously defended[5]) the 'people of the holy ones of Elyon' who appear in the interpretation of ch. 7's vision (7.27) correspond to the humanoid symbol. But another line of interpretation takes the humanoid figure to be a heavenly being.[6] In support of this view are three main considerations. One is the suggestion of J. Emerton that behind the vision lies a Canaanite mythical scene in which the god El bequeaths power to the younger god Baal.[7] The name 'ancient of days' is very similar to El's epithet 'father of years' ('*b šnym*) in the Ugaritic corpus, and Baal is, like this human figure, depicted in Canaanite myth as occasionally travelling on clouds.[8] The

5.    *Daniel*, pp. 100-108. This is also the view of C.H.W. Brekelmans, 'The Saints of the Most High and their Kingdom', *OTS* 14 (1965), pp. 305-29; G.F. Hasel, 'The Identity of the "Saints of the Most High" in Daniel 7', *Bib* 56 (1975), pp. 173-92; L. Hartman and A.A. DiLella, *The Book of Daniel* (AB; New York: Doubleday, 1977), pp. 85-102.

6.    The major proponents of this view have been M. Noth, 'The Holy Ones of the Most High', in *The Laws in the Pentateuch and Other Essays* (Philadelphia: Fortress Press, 1967), pp. 215-28; L. Dequeker, 'The "Saints of the Most High" in Qumran and Daniel', *OTS* 18 (1973), pp. 133-62; and J.J. Collins, *The Apocalyptic Vision of the Book of Daniel* (Missoula, MT: Scholars Press, 1977), pp. 123-47, 167-84, and Collins, *Daniel*, pp. 304-10, 312-19.

7.    J.A. Emerton, 'The Origin of the Son of Man Imagery', *JTS* 9 (1958), pp. 225-42.

8.    Dan. 7.13; for a discussion of the Ugaritic background, see also A.J. Ferch,

second consideration is the phrase 'holy ones' which, it is argued, refers almost overwhelmingly to heavenly beings in the Jewish scriptures and in other Jewish literature of the Second Temple period. The third is the appearance of Michael in ch. 12, possibly playing the role allotted to this figure.

Seen from a historical-critical perspective, the answer to this problem may be that the understanding of the humanoid figure in ch. 7 has changed during the process of evolution of the book of Daniel. Certainly, if, as has been suggested,[9] ch. 7 at one stage stood with chs. 2–6 and without chs. 8–12, it seems to me (still) that the 'symbolic' interpretation carries considerable weight. We have no other heavenly figures in these chapters, save for the enigmatic 'fourth person' who has 'the appearance of a divine being' in the middle of the furnace (3.23). However, the point at issue here is how one reads ch. 7 in the light of what was included in Daniel after it was written.

If we are to read from the perspective of the MT book as a whole, then, we must resolve the questions of ch. 7 by asking what happens after it: where does sovereignty go? There is no doubt that it rests firmly with heavenly beings who are much in evidence in the final chapters. Chapters 8–12 also make it clear that the sovereignty of Elyon is not to be delegated but transferred, since the old god makes no active reappearance and plays no part in the hoped-for resolution hinted at in ch. 12. Is the scene of ch. 7 to be located, then, at the end of history, as ch. 2 would suggest? If that is so, do the 'princes' (שׂרים), the junior deities, assume the governance of the world throughout chs. 8–12? Or is ch. 7 in exactly the right place, marking not a deferred resolution but a real-time shift?

For on either side of ch. 7 lie two dispensations, the 'before' and 'after', the rule of the old bearded and white-haired Elyon,[10] and the rule of the new humanoid being. The book makes the contrast between these two halves of eternity quite clear. The contents of chs. 1–6 portray an essentially ordered cosmos, presided over by the divine lord of history, the old Elyon, who is, as Nebuchadnezzar says, 'god of gods

'Daniel 7 and Ugarit: A Reconsideration', *JBL* 99 (1980), pp. 75-86.

9.    See Noth, 'The Holy Ones of the Most High'; P. Lenglet, 'La structure littéraire de Daniel 2–7', *Bib* 53 (1972), pp. 169-90; Collins, *Apocalyptic Vision*, pp. 11-14.

10.    The title עליא found at 7.25 (twice) recurs in 3.26, 32; 4.14, 21-22, 29, 31; 5.18, 21; 6.11 (verses according to Aramaic text).

and lord of kings, and a revealer of mysteries' (2.47), and who, as Daniel says, 'removes kings and sets up kings; he gives wisdom to the wise and knowledge to those who have understanding' (2.21). Elyon runs the world as a monarch, appointing kings, causing them to be instructed and corrected when necessary, and rescuing his own wise servants when they need it. It is a pretty orderly and well-run universe. In every case, except one, the ruler whom Elyon has appointed comes, at the end of the episode, to realize his own circumscribed role and status in the scheme of things, and to acknowledge the sovereignty of this one deity. On the one occasion, in ch. 5, when a human king exceeds his bounds by too much, Elyon terminates his contract abruptly and permanently.

The contrast with the state of affairs in chs. 8–12 is dramatic. Here the orderly sequence of world rulers under a single deity who is the lord of history disappears. Unlike Darius the Mede, these rulers do not 'receive the kingdom'. Indeed, the language of 'one kingdom' residing in the high god no longer functions. We meet instead bestial kings, successively more powerful and wicked, who rise from a chaotic sea, as in ch. 7, confront one another like a ram and a goat (as in ch. 8) or as king of north and south respectively (in ch. 11), the latest of whom even challenges the authority of the heavenly realm. And, importantly, note that this opposition does not name Elyon: these kings 'grow great, even to the *host of heaven*' (8.10).

But this is only part of the picture. Why are these rulers, who in the opening chapters have been brought to heel, and whom in ch. 7 Elyon has judged and sentenced, able to mount this challenge? The answer is that Elyon is no longer the 'lord of heaven', the monarch of the universe. The heavenly realm itself is involved in the struggle for power. The conflict between the empires of Persia and Greece is not merely an earthly one, but is led by their heavenly protagonists, their 'princes' (10.20-21). There is war between the gods. Disorder on earth is matched by (caused by?) disorder in heaven. And where is the supreme god who exercises final control? Where, indeed? He is simply *not there*. We look in vain after ch. 7 for the great Elyon whose orderly rule over the cosmos characterized the earlier chapters. The only voices we hear and the only bodies we now see are those of other supernatural beings. At their head is no longer Elyon, but one of the heavenly beings with the title 'prince of princes' (שׂר־שׂרים, 8.25). And he is not named; perhaps the office is vacant? But where did the office come from in the first place? It is now evident that the placing of the 'thrones' (note the plural) in 7.9 alerts us to the sovereignty of several other divine beings. Perhaps in theory there was always a 'divine council'—but if so, its members were inactive until old Elyon decided to step down.

In ch. 9 Daniel, perhaps still convalescing from the sickness that had overcome him and remaining 'dismayed by the vision' (8.27)[11] looks back in his books to a prophecy of Jeremiah about the length of the devastation of Jerusalem. Daniel has not previously looked for answers. His interpretations have been sought from him, and his visions come to him unasked. But here he actively looks for the solution to a puzzle he has found. The new history he has been granted to see is not the history that Elyon had promised. Insecurity sets in: he looks up previous words from his god (Yhwh, v. 2) and finds himself perplexed. He doubts the one thing he had always maintained: history was under his god's control. And so for the first time his confidence wavers. Are such promises conditional? Is it possible that the future is not decreed, but there stands some obstacle? For the only time in the book of Daniel we find a breach in the facade of its deterministic ideology: Daniel confesses sin, and in so doing acknowledges that the divine punishment was caused by his people's disobedience. Human behaviour can, after all, determine the outcome of history. And so contrition is in order, and, following that, *a request for action*. For Daniel the time is already fulfilled and the plan has not come about. There is a crisis here. Can resorting to the familiar old Deuteronomistic language of Israel's wilfulness, deserved punishment, necessary repentance, somehow bring back the old order to which it referred? On this interpretation, ch. 9 is not anomalous, not an enigma. It is a wistful, even nostalgic yearning for the old order.

To whom does Daniel pray? He does not address Elyon by name, but uses the term 'lord' (אדני, vv. 3, 4, 7, 15, 16, 17, 19; in v. 3 the deity is referred to as אדני אלהים). Why this language? Perhaps Daniel does not know to whom he should address his petition any more. Or perhaps he alludes to the opening of his book, where the term occurs for the only time outside ch. 9: ויתן אדני בידו את־יהויקים מלך־יהודה 'and *Adonay* handed over into his power Jehoiakim king of Judah' (1.2). What more appropriate term with which to address the deity responsible for *Heilsgeschichte*? Did *Adonay* give him an answer? Well, even as Daniel speaks, a divine being comes along, claiming to bring the word (he does

11. Remember that in the book's chronological scheme (5.31) Darius succeeds Belshazzar!

not say from whom: the phrase is דבר יצא, 'a word came out'). No longer, then, the word from the deity himself, but from the same source that had provided the troubling explanation relayed in ch. 8. Instead of the action he asks for (v. 19) from the god in charge, what he gets is a visit from one of the management team explaining why nothing can be done yet!

This procedure continues to the end of the book. Instead of the revelations and interventions from Elyon which are the feature of chs. 2–6, we get explanations from heavenly beings in human form, beings whose existence had been concealed in the first part of the book. It is now *they*, and not Elyon, who reveal what is to come in the future. It is they, after all, who are shaping the future by their struggles with each other. And this dramatic change in the population, constitution and conduct of the heavenly realm means that the authority of the divine decree is replaced by the authority of military force, hierarchy by anarchy, order by chaos. Might is right, but no longer is there a god with a monopoly of power. Monarchy is dead, and the universe is run by warring beings, whether humans on earth or gods in human form in heaven. The cosmos has lost its ruler, and history has consequently lost its author and its meaning. This is what moderns might call the 'death of God'.

This loss of meaning is particularly important. Instead of the definitive *action* of chs. 1–6 we now find *promises* in 7–12. There is, of course, a series of assurances, even predictions, about the happy ending to the violent course which history has now taken. But the promises do not inspire confidence. We are perhaps reminded of the sequence of promises made to Abraham, dealt with in Chapter 4. But there at least Abraham had no doubt of whom he was dealing with, nor, ultimately, of the ability of Yhwh to get his way if he really insisted. Here there is no Yhwh, not even an Elyon, in sole charge, and the issue is not whether one can trust the intentions of the promising deity but whether the promising deity has the power or competence to deliver. In ch. 7 the promise, made on behalf of Elyon, is that the 'people of the holy ones of Elyon' will receive an everlasting kingdom', along the lines of Elyon's original plan in ch. 2. Perhaps that original plan is still theoretically in force. But in 8.25 the vision ends rather less rosily. The 'great horn' will be destroyed without human agency, but this phrase resembles little more than a hint of the stone of ch. 2, and nothing further is said about what will follow his defeat; nothing about a new kingdom, certainly. In ch. 9, too, after much distress, the desolator will receive his 'decreed end'. But no details can be given at this stage. With the focus on the motif of destruction, the language of violence is, nevertheless, characteristic of the new regime, and disturbingly so. It is the language of warriors whose goal is retribution, destruction, victory, the elimination of the opponent. Where is the language of administration, of peace, of stability, of *order*? There are no such promises, and the vision of the future does not extend so far as to sketch out any rehabilitated world. And so we finally we come to ch. 12. Here the plot impels the author to confront with some degree of explicitness what is actually projected to take place. But far from stamping a final and definitive seal on the world's history and on Daniel's book, this closing chapter leaves the disturbing impression that the future is not clearly foreseen. Michael will 'arise' (עמד: scholars argue about what exactly this verb means here, and perhaps it is intended by the author to be as vague as possible). And who is this Michael anyway? Neither we nor Daniel have met him before. Whence his authority? We learn that he is in charge of Daniel's people. Did Daniel know this already, or is he just learning something new? Is this Michael Elyon's successor? Is he the human figure of ch. 7? Neither Daniel nor we are told. We are informed only that his presence will bring a time of trouble. Why trouble, and from which quarter? One could not imagine the old Elyon countenancing 'trouble' for *his* people. He was in the business of delivering.

But then, Elyon was managing the history of the world, and his plan had been to end the sequence of empires with a permanent settlement. That plan has obviously been abandoned. The new solution foresees a quite different outcome. First, the good news: 'your people will be delivered'; now the bad news: 'all those whose names are written in the book'! This bureaucratic qualification leaves the assurance of deliverance rather empty, for who has seen the book, and who keeps it? Not all of Elyon's chosen people, apparently, are going to get the kingdom they were once promised. But here is more news: they are not going to get a kingdom at all! A different kind of solution to the degenerating historical process has been planned. Some humans will be rewarded with eternal life, some eternal damnation. Resurrection and judgment of humans, of course, had never been part of Elyon's plan. Chapter 7 witnesses the power of the earthly empires being removed, but the job was not finished, for 'their existence was extended for a season and a time' (7.12). Unfinished business, indeed! The device of bringing back some dead people to a vaguely worded reward and punishment has all the appearance of a measure designed to compensate for the failure to achieve a just and orderly *world* administration. History has got into such a mess that it is now better to abandon it altogether. As a result of horrendous deeds that have remained unpunished and deaths that were undeserved, the heavenly rulers of the new order are undertaking to put things right posthumously by bringing back to life those needing reward or punishment and meting out the appropriate retribution. It is not clear, though, whether the intention is to deal with everyone or just those with whom the deities have unfinished business, victims or perpetrators of evil.[12] The wording seems to imply that only certain people are going to merit special treatment: the 'wise'.

And, we also want to know (as Daniel himself has persistently asked), when will the solution come? Notoriously, the book gives us cryptic and contradictory answers: three and a half times; 1290 days; 1335 days. Those keeping the 'book' with the names in are not very good clerks when it comes to timekeeping. This promised end has no fixed date! Daniel writes, 'I heard him swear by the one who lives forever that it would be for three and a half times', and he adds, 'I heard but could not understand, so I said, "My lord, what will be the outcome of these things?"' (12.7-8). What Daniel did not understand we are not told. Perhaps he was unsure of the three and a half times; perhaps he no longer knew who was 'the one that lives forever'—the absent Elyon, present only as a name to be invoked by an unreliable divine bureaucrat? The device of having the sage ask a question is common in apocalyptic literature, and it logically leads to the explanation that the reader needs to be offered. But here Daniel's request is *not* met. He is told, 'On your way, Daniel...' and given more cryptic assurances that the wise will understand and the foolish will not. This is repeated with the added advice that he might as well die (12.13, 'on your way and rest; you shall arise for your reward at the end of the days'). And where does it leave the reader? None of us wants to admit to not understanding, because that means we are foolish. So we all pretend to understand this rigmarole. But what is there to understand?

There are, then, a host of features in this short final chapter that undermine the confidence conveyed earlier in the book that history was under control, and that active intervention from a god in charge could be relied upon. Now, not only is history in chaos, but the plans for the

12. The term רבים, which means 'many' may apparently be used to render 'all'.

future seem also to be uncertain and unreliable; there is only an assurance that at some time in the future some people would be raised from the dead. The reader, like Daniel, can only wait in hope that those running history and the world can get their act together.

What, then, was depicted in ch. 7? What explains the stark contrast between the chapters preceding that vision and those that follow it? As I observed earlier, what takes place is a rupture in the fabric of eternity, a sudden change in the administration of history. It is impossible to read Daniel coherently if the vision of ch. 7 relates to the end of history and promises a final abiding kingdom. However that vision might once have been read, its significance has been determined by subsequent chapters.

Looking back at ch. 7 from the end of ch. 12, one can only come to the realization that what took place there was an act of abdication. Perhaps Daniel realized it at the time. When he saw the transfer of power from old autocrat to an unnamed humanlike figure, he said, 'my spirit within me was anxious and the visions of my head alarmed me'. With good reason, we might add! What the wise seer was witnessing is effectively the 'death of god', which will result in the collapse of order, the intensification of conflict on earth and the advent of conflict in heaven.

This vision was not, indeed, one of an event at the end of history, but occurred at a moment *in* history, the narrative moment between chs. 6 and 8. *From that moment onwards*, Elyon is no longer directing history. He is effectively dead. His name may be invoked as the one who lives forever but all power has been shed. And with this abdication comes an abandonment of all his plans. To Daniel his successors can offer promises, even proffer differing timescales. But these all confirm that the plans of Elyon are no longer operative, betray confusion and lack of direction, and hint at incompetence in world management. Whatever they may purpose for the future, in the present they fight it out between themselves while earthly kings run riot. The great sea from which the bestial empires arise in ch. 7 rages on until the end of the book and beyond. I do not see that one can read the book of Daniel as an optimistic work, and I do not get a feeling that the authors who bequeathed it to us in this form were deeply committed to the prospect of everything turning out all right in the end.

Let us consider for a moment the question of 'authorial intent'. What I have been doing so far is a 'final form' reading. Yet I have already suggested that the meaning of the vision in ch. 7 may have changed as the final chapters were added. Whether or not a deliberate reinterpretation of the chapter took place, the vision of the world and its history that the authors of chs. 8–12 overlaid onto the preceding material inevitably shaped the perception of that material. It is quite appropriate, then, to move from a 'final form' reading to a consideration of the ideology of the authors of chs. 8–12 who are also responsible for having shaped the way in which the entire book, including ch. 7, is to be read. After all (if the reader needs further reminding), it is human authors who have decided to portray Elyon as having been in charge of history, and human authors who have scripted his departure from the plot. The 'death of god' is a *narrative* event (like every other thing that he does in biblical texts).

How did the authors of Daniel comprehend their own times, upon which they were obviously trying to comment? Like Daniel in ch. 9, they may continue to pray to 'God' (אדני אלהים), but they have written him out of the script, and they do not lead us, the readers, to think that anyone in overall charge is listening to Daniel (or them?) They do not foresee the rebirth of the old monarchic god of order, nor a return to the old system. There is no final kingdom of the chosen people. Indeed, there *is* no 'chosen people', there are only 'chosen individuals', the wise like Daniel. The nation itself is hopelessly divided into righteous and wicked. Only individual wise people are left to hope for anything at all.

They do, however, include themselves among those righteous, for they surely are those who 'turn many to righteousness' and who will 'shine like the brightness of the sky' and be 'like the stars for ever' (12.3). Their names are certainly written in the book. For the new order is not so unlike the old order in one respect. The elite will always win through. Just as Daniel's piety did not debar him from political honours in the court of the foreign king, neither will the righteousness of this elite be prevented from holding high office in whatever regime may finally supervene.[13]

Is this interpretation of the book of Daniel purely a wishful anti-reading of a twentieth-century cynic, or even a mere mischief-maker? To anyone for whom there must be a 'biblical' view of history, and that view must be ultimately optimistic, the idea that Judaean writers might ever speculate that their god was dead, and history was in the power of

---

13. I have explored this theme in 'Reading Daniel Sociologically', in A.S. van der Woude (ed.), *The Book of Daniel in the Light of New Findings* (BETL, 106; Leuven: Peeters, 1993), pp. 345-61.

irresponsible forces could never occur. If such people had ever wanted to write such an idea down for posterity, the canonizers and the canonical critics will do their best to make sure that message gets drowned in the rosy glow of more pious sentiments elsewhere in their bible. There are things ancient Judaean writers simply cannot be allowed to say, because now that they have been deemed to have written scripture, they have to behave; if they have misbehaved they have to be glossed by editors of their own time (Qoheleth) or have their mischief exegeted away.

I have no idea whether I am reading the minds of the writers of Daniel, of those, I mean, that left us the Masoretic form. But I certainly do not rule out the possibility that they may have wished to communicate what I am hearing. And if this is what they wished to communicate, then why? I am obliged to suggest some account of their identity and motivation.

Does the book of Daniel emerge from the ideological values and the historical experience of the authors, their individual psyches, their class, their society? If so (and it is an 'if') their book may tell us this about them. They remember, really or in imagination, a time when there was a clear demarcation between gods and humans, with kingship quite distinctly on the human side (regardless of what kings may have tried to claim). Now they live in a world in which deities take human form, human kings behave like gods and gods like human kings: that is, their business is warfare, the establishment of sovereignty over their fellow monarchs or gods.

Is this a recognizable portrait of the mid-second century BCE? Much has been written of the conflict between the ancient Near Eastern perception of society and the Greek perception. The Greeks did not accord cults and religions the same political influence that they enjoyed further east. Now, the background to the book of Daniel is generally seen as being a crisis within Judah brought about by competing ideologies, often represented as 'traditional' on the one hand and 'Hellenistic' on the other. I am aware that discussion of this issue has often been oversimplistic. But the book of Daniel does tell the story of the death of an old authoritarian, autocratic, but essentially benign world order, and takes a pessimistic view of the overthrow of this traditional order by a society consisting of powerful and competing states and deities, the deities clothed in suspiciously human form.

And what of the individualism which clearly emerges in Daniel? Perhaps the hero is, like his companions, in a way a model of the pious Judaean, at least to start with. But the picture of a people clearly distinguished as an ethnic minority, with a distinct and homogeneous religion and awaiting their final turn at inheriting the worldwide kingdom of Elyon does not survive the second half of the book. The great empires are, by the time of the writers of chs. 8–12, long gone, replaced by smaller monarchies, cities, colonies. Correspondingly, the inhabitants of Judah no longer constitute a single society. I am not saying that they ever did; the authors of Daniel are quite probably harking back to a past which in several respects is of their own wishing. I gain the impression, nevertheless, that they are disillusioned by what they see as a world that has lost its sense, in which they have no longer any faith. They can still hope for some kind of justice, for some gesture of theodicy in a post-mortem vindication, but hope, rather than confidence, it remains, its details and timing unclear. They aspire, of course, to be among the saved, they still believe in elites (to which they belong); they belong, perhaps, no longer to the earthly elite but hope to make the heavenly one.[14] They are, I surmise, an ex-elite, grumpy, disenchanted, feeling persecuted, their 'wisdom' unwanted. They read the signs of their times, and the verdict is bad. Like their wise old god, these wise old men (or so they see themselves) belong to an order that is past.

Now it is time to replace the *explicatio* with *applicatio*. What does a modern get from this old book? There are two interesting paths leading from the reading I have just offered. One points towards our own time. There are those who in every age have read the book in a more optimistic light, grasping one solution, one decoded message after another: the book points to Jesus Christ, or to the Christian church, or the conversion of Constantine, or the millennium, or whatever has not yet been disproved. There still remain readers, probably a majority, who believe that the world order is still the one apparent in chs. 1–6 rather than 7–12. These are people who profess faith in cosmic order, in a future that is preordained. For these people there remains a stable transcendental authority, and for them the instructions are those given to Daniel: 'wait (and take your calculator with you if you like)'.

There are others who still cannot imagine what they could have preached at Auschwitz and Belsen, who look with dismay at continual

14. I have explored the psychology of the authors more fully in 'Reading Daniel Sociologically'.

political atrocities, at governments who connive with torture and ethnic cleansing, at nations and corporations whose power to wreck the earth, wreck human freedom and destroy life seems unchecked by any transcendental court of justice, who experience exactly those feelings that I have imputed to the book's producers, the *maskilim*. I do not claim to be one, but neither do I recognize the world in which *I* live as being governed by a powerful and benign transcendental monarch. The book of Daniel makes sense to me in a way that the usual readings of it do not.

There are other readers who, more than I, have been vulnerable to the values of postmodernity. They see authority, hope, value as all irredeemably outmoded, or as corroded by the rust of deconstruction. In the postmodern world pluralism also reigns. Decree is replaced by negotiation. The tyranny of the majority is smashed by the tyranny of minorities. Language cannot refer to anything outside of itself. The fulfilment of desire can only ever be deferred. Without the old white-haired Elyon-type god how *can* there be objectivity or value? Daniel can indeed be read as a highly postmodern text, a celebration, if that is the word, of the dispersal of authority, and with it the abolition of any certain knowledge, of confidence and of determinate meaning, even of history as a process rather than a sequence. The only difference from Daniel is that the world is ruled not by deities in human guise but by humans acting like deities.

Is this reading of Daniel in danger of being seen as a very reactionary and middle-aged paper? Like the authors of Daniel, I see in history and in texts the story that I want to see. I like to think they were middle-aged too. Certainly I belong to a class and profession that can be compared with theirs as far as any comparison at all can be made. I enjoy the conceit that I have shared something of an anxiety over the departure of a world of values that is irrecoverable. I hope I am more optimistic than they about the future of human society—I can afford to be, since no-one is persecuting me. My privileges are not being seriously threatened. But, like them, I shall have to wait and see whether the future is worth hoping for, and meanwhile try and make sense of it all by my own literary efforts. I do not expect any supernatural assurances, and I would not believe any of them anyway. But I do recognize that my own nostalgia and twinges of unease about the future resonate with what I find in Daniel (and thus make me suspicious of my own eisegesis).

I also see, however, that these ancient elite intellectuals are no more authorized to speak for their own people than I am for other readers of the book of Daniel. I have no doubt that in the second century BCE there were Judaeans who revelled in the exciting new multicultural world in which the heritages of the great civilizations were being traded in an increasingly open market and an increasingly accessible Hellenistic cultural currency. The Romans, after all, did also bring stability, if not the kind that many Judaeans liked. Nowadays, too, there must be among the readers of Daniel those who will respond to a world governed by the younger generation of gods, who celebrate the freedom gained by the abolition of the old dictator and find in the conflict that follows the seeds of a brighter future after all. In the end, we probably all tend to find in these biblical texts something that we want. But if we can keep our wants as free as possible, there is the chance that the process of reading will reverse and the text will draw some meaning from the reader.

And that is when it matters very much 'whose bible it is'.

# BIBLIOGRAPHY

Albertz, R., *A History of Israelite Religion in the Old Testament Period*. I. *From the Beginnings to the End of the Exile* (London: SCM Press, 1994).

Althusser, L., 'Ideology and Ideological State Apparatuses', in *Lenin and Philosophy and Other Essays* (New York: Monthly Review Press, 1971).

Baines, J., 'Literacy and Ancient Egyptian Society', in *Man* (London: Royal Anthropological Institute of Great Britain and Ireland, 1983), pp. 572-99.

Baker, D.L., *Two Testaments, One Bible* (Leicester: Lutterworth, 1976).

Barr, J., *Does Biblical Study still Belong to Theology?* (Oxford: Clarendon Press, 1978).

—*Holy Scripture: Canon, Authority, Criticism* (Oxford: Clarendon Press, 1983).

Barton, J., *Oracles of God: Perceptions of Ancient Prophecy after the Exile* (London: Darton, Longman & Todd, 1986).

—'Should Old Testament Study be more Theological', *ExpTim* 100 (1989), pp. 443-48.

—*What is the Bible* (London: SPCK, 1991).

Begrich, J., 'Das priesterliche Heilsorakel', *ZAW* 52 (1934), pp. 81-92.

Brekelmans, C.H.W., 'The Saints of the Most High and their Kingdom', *OTS* 14 (1965), pp. 305-29.

Brett, M.G., 'Four or Five Things to Do with Texts', in Clines *et al.* (eds.), *The Bible in Three Dimensions*, pp. 357-77.

—*Biblical Criticism in Crisis? The Impact of the Canonical Approach on Old Testament Studies* (Cambridge: Cambridge University Press, 1991).

Broyles, C.C., *The Conflict of Faith and Experience in the Psalms: A Form-Critical Theological Study* (JSOTSup, 52; Sheffield: JSOT Press, 1989).

Calvert, N.C., 'Abraham Traditions in Middle Jewish Literature: Implications for the Interpretation of Galatians and Romans' (PhD thesis, University of Sheffield, 1993).

*The Cambridge History of the Bible* (3 vols.; Cambridge: Cambridge University Press, 1963–70).

Childs, B., *Introduction to the Old Testament as Scripture* (Philadelphia: Westminster Press; London: SCM Press, 1979).

Clines, D.J.A., *What Does Eve Do to Help? and Other Readerly Questions to the Old Testament* (JSOTSup, 94 Sheffield: JSOT Press, 1990).

Clines, D.J.A., S.A. Fowl and S.E. Porter (eds.), *The Bible in Three Dimensions: Essays in Celebration of Forty Years of Biblical Studies in the University of Sheffield* (JSOTSup, 87; Sheffield: JSOT Press, 1990).

Collins, J.J., *The Apocalyptic Vision of the Book of Daniel* (Missoula, MT: Scholars Press, 1977).

—*Daniel* (Hermeneia; Minneapolis: Fortress Press, 1993).

Davies, P.R., *Daniel* (OTG; Sheffield: JSOT Press, 1985).

—'Do Old Testament Studies Need a Dictionary', in Clines *et al.* (eds.), *The Bible in Three Dimensions*, pp. 321-25.

—'Reading Daniel Sociologically', in A.S. van der Woude (ed.), *The Book of Daniel in the Light of New Findings* (BETL, 106; Leuven: Peeters, 1993), pp. 345-61.

—*In Search of Ancient Israel* (JSOTSup, 148; repr.;. Sheffield: Sheffield Academic Press, 1995).

Demsky, A., and M. Bar-Ilan, 'Writing in Ancient Israel and Early Judaism', in M.J. Mulder (ed.), *Miqra* (CRINT; Assen: Van Gorcum; Philadelphia: Fortress Press, 1988), pp. 1-38.

Dequeker, L.,'The "Saints of the Most High" in Qumran and Daniel', *OTS* 18 (1973), pp. 133-62.

Dentan, R.C., *Preface to Old Testament Theology* (New York: Seabury Press, 2nd edn 1963 [1950]).

Dyck, J., 'The Purpose of Chronicles and the Critique of Ideology' (PhD thesis, University of Sheffield, 1994).

Emerton, J.A., 'The Origin of the Son of Man Imagery', *JTS* 9 (1958), pp. 225-42.

Evans, C.F., *Explorations in Theology 2* (London: SCM Press, 1987).

—*'Is Holy Scripture Christian?' and Other Questions* (London: SCM Press, 1971).

Exum, J.C., *Fragmented Women: Feminist (Sub)versions of Biblical Narratives* (JSOTSup, 163; Sheffield: JSOT Press, 1993).

Ferch, A.J., 'Daniel 7 and Ugarit: A Reconsideration', *JBL* 99 (1980), pp. 75-86.

Ferguson, E., 'Canon Muratori: Date and Provenance', *Studia Patristica* 18 (1982), pp. 677-83.

Foucault, M., *The Archaeology of Knowledge* (New York: Harper & Row, 1972).

Fox, R.L., *The Unauthorized Version: Truth and Fiction in the Bible* (London: Viking Press, 1991).

Frye, N., *The Great Code: The Bible and Literature* (Toronto: Academic Press of Canada, 1983).

Gadamer, H.-G., *Truth and Method* (New York: Seabury Press, 1975).

Gerstenberger, E., *Der bittende Mensch* (Neukirchen: Neukirchener Verlag, 1980).

Godelier, J., 'Infrastructure, Societies and History', *Current Anthropology* 19 (1978), pp. 763-68.

Goldingay, J., *Daniel* (WBC; Dallas: Word Books, 1989).

Goshen-Gottstein, M.H., *The Hebrew University Bible, the Book of Isaiah, Vols I–II* (Jerusalem: Hebrew Bible Project, 1975, 1981).

Gunn, D.M., 'Reading Right: Reliable and Omniscient Narrator, Omniscient God and Foolproof Composition', in Clines *et al.* (eds.), *The Bible in Three Dimensions*, pp. 53-64.

Gunn, D.M., and D.N. Fewell, *Narrative in the Hebrew Bible* (Oxford: Oxford University Press, 1993).

Habermas, J., *Knowledge and Human Interests* (Boston: Beacon Press, 1975).

Harris, M., *Cultural Materialism: The Struggle for a Science of Culture* (New York: Vintage Books, 1979).

Hartman, L., and A.A. DiLella, *The Book of Daniel* (AB; New York: Doubleday, 1977), pp. 85-102.

Hasel, G.F., 'The Identity of the "Saints of the Most High" in Daniel 7', *Bib* 56 (1975), pp. 173-92.

—*Old Testament Theology: Basic Issues in the Current Debate* (Grand Rapids: Eerdmans, 4th edn, 1991).

Headland, T.N., K.L. Pike and M. Harris, *Emics and Etics: The Insider/Outside Debate* (Frontiers of Anthropology, 7; Newbury Park: Sage Publications, 1990).

Horsley, R.A., *Jesus and the Spiral of Violence: Popular Jewish Resistance in Roman Palestine* (Minneapolis: Fortress Press, 1993).

Kenyon, F.G., *The Story of the Bible* (London: John Murray, 2nd edn, 1964).

Koch, K., 'Gibt es ein Vergeltungsdogma im AT?', *ZTK* 52 (1955), pp. 1-42.

Kraus, H.-J., *Die biblische Theologie: Ihre Geschichte und Problematik* (Neukirchen–Vluyn: Neukirchener Verlag, 1970).

Kubo, A., and W.F. Specht, *So Many Versions? 20th Century English Versions of the Bible* (revised and enlarged edition; Grand Rapids: Zondervan, 1983).

Kvanvig, H., *Roots of Apocalyptic: The Mesopotamian Background of the Enoch Figure and of the Son of Man* (WMANT; Neukirchen–Vluyn: Neukirchener Verlag, 1988).

Lenglet, P., 'La structure littéraire de Daniel 2–7', *Bib* 53 (1972), pp. 169-90.

Lust, J., 'The Septuagint Version of Daniel 4–5', in A.S. van der Woude (ed.), *The Book of Daniel in the Light of New Findings* (BETL, 106; Leuven: Peeters, 1993), pp. 39-53

Marx, K., and F. Engels, *Marx and Engels on Religion* (New York: Schocken Books, 1964).

Millard, A., 'An Assessment of the Evidence for Writing in Ancient Israel', in *Biblical Archaeology Today* (Jerusalem: Israel Exploration Society and Israel Academy of Sciences in association with the American Schools of Oriental Research, 1985), pp. 301-12.

Miller, J.W., *The Origins of the Bible* (New York; Paulist Press, 1994).

Miscall, P.D., *The Workings of Old Testament Narrative* (Philadelphia: Fortress Press; Chico, CA: Scholars Press, 1983).

Moberly, R.W.L., *From Eden to Golgotha: Essays in Biblical Theology* (Atlanta: Scholars Press, 1992).

Nida, E.A., and C.R. Taber, *The Theory and Practice of Translation* (Helps for Translators, 8; Leiden: Brill, 1969).

Noth, M., 'The Holy Ones of the Most High', in *The Laws in the Pentateuch and Other Essays* (Philadelphia: Fortress Press, 1967), pp. 215-28.

Pattie, T.S., *Manuscripts of the Bible* (London: The British Library, 1979).

Petersen, D.L., 'A Thrice-Told Tale: Genre, Theme and Motif', *BR* 18 (1973), pp. 30-43.

Pike, K., 'Towards a Theory of the Structure of Human Behavior', in D. Hymes (ed.), *Language in Culture and Society* (New York: Harper & Row, 1964), pp. 154-61.

Preuss, H.D., *Theologie des Alten Testaments. I. JHWHs erwählendes und verplichtendes Handeln* (Stuttgart: Kohlhammer, 1991).

Rashkow, I., *The Phallacy of Genesis: A Feminist-Psychoanalytical Approach* (Literary Currents in Biblical Interpretation; Louisville: Westminster/John Knox, 1993).

Reventlow, H. Graf, *Problems of Old Testament Theology in the Twentieth Century* (London: SCM Press, 1985).

Ricoeur, P., *Time and Narrative* (3 vols.; Chicago: Chicago University Press, 1984–88).

Roberts, C.H., and T.C. Skeat, *The Birth of the Codex* (London: The British Academy, 1983).

Rogerson, J.W., and P.R. Davies, *The Old Testament World* (Cambridge: Cambridge University Press; Englewood Cliffs, NJ: Prentice-Hall, 1989).

Sanders, J.A., *From Sacred Text to Sacred Story* (Philadelphia: Fortress Press, 1987).

Sawyer, J.F.A., *From Moses to Patmos: New Perspectives in Old Testament Study* (London: SPCK, 1977).

—'The Image of God, the Wisdom of Serpents and the Knowledge of Good and Evil', in P. Morris and D. Sawyer (eds.), *A Walk in the Garden: Biblical, Iconographical and Literary Images of Eden* (JSOTSup, 136; Sheffield: JSOT Press, 1992).

Seybold, K., *Introducing the Psalms* (ET; Edinburgh: T. & T. Clark, 1990), pp. 82-85.

Skeat, T.C., 'Early Christian Book-Production: Papyri and Manuscripts', in *The Cambridge History of the Bible*. II. *The West From the Fathers to the Reformation* (Cambridge: Cambridge University Press, 1969), pp. 54-79.

Spiegel, S., *The Last Trial* (trans. J. Goldin; New York: Random House, 1967).

Sternberg, M., *The Poetics of Biblical Narrative: Ideological Literature and the Drama of Reading* (Bloomington: Indiana University Press, 1985).

Sternberg, N., *Kinship and Marriage in Genesis: A Household Economics Perspective* (Minneapolis: Fortress Press, 1993).

Sundberg, A., 'Canon Muratori: A Fourth Century list', *HTR* 66 (1973), pp. 1-41.

Thompson, T.L., *The Origin Tradition of Ancient Israel* (JSOTSup, 55; Sheffield: JSOT Press, 1987).

Tov, E., *Textual Criticism of the Hebrew Bible* (Minneapolis: Fortress Press, 1992).

Turner, L., *Announcements of Plot in Genesis* (JSOTSup, 96; Sheffield: JSOT Press, 1990).

Watson, F., *Text, Church and World* (Edinburgh: T. & T. Clark; Grand Rapids: Eerdmans, 1994).

Weber, M., *The Sociology of Religion* (ET; New York: Beacon Press, 1963).

Westermann, C., *Praise and Lament in the Psalms* (Edinburgh: T. & T. Clark, 1981).

Wilder, A., *Jesus' Parables and the War of Myths: Essays on Imagination in the Scripture* (ed. J. Breech; Philadelphia: Fortress Press, 1982).

Wilson, G.H., *The Editing of the Hebrew Psalter* (Chico, CA: Scholars Press, 1983).

Zindler, F., *Dial an Atheist* (Austin: American Atheist Press, 1991).

# INDEXES

## INDEX OF REFERENCES

| | | | | | | | |
|---|---|---|---|---|---|---|---|
| *Ecclesiasticus* | | *2 Corinthians* | | *Revelation* | | |
| 24.23 | 59 | 11.3 | 90 | 5.1 | 86 | |
| | | | | 21 | 71 | |
| New Testament | | *Galatians* | | 22 | 71 | |
| *Matthew* | | 3.6-9 | 95 | | | |
| 24.34 | 68 | 3.6 | 105 | Pseudepigrapha | | |
| | | | | *4 Ezra* | | |
| *Mark* | | *1 Timothy* | | 14.45 | 60 | |
| 12.13-17 | 52 | 2.11-15 | 90 | | | |
| 15.34 | 115 | | | Josephus | | |
| | | *Hebrews* | | *Apion* | | |
| *Luke* | | 9 | 76 | 1.37-43 | 60 | |
| 1.46-55 | 125 | 11 | 95 | | | |
| 3.38 | 93 | | | Classical | | |
| | | *James* | | *Martial* | | |
| *Romans* | | 2.21-24 | 95 | 1.2 | 62 | |
| 4 | 95 | | | | | |

# INDEX OF AUTHORS

# JOURNAL FOR THE STUDY OF THE OLD TESTAMENT

## Supplement Series